A TEMP [illegible] D
DREAM

Edited by Hina Babar.

Cover illustration by Ben Jackson.

Map illustration by Melissa Nash.

PRAISE FOR A TEMPEST OF EMERALD DREAM

An absorbing fantasy adventure with a colourful world, diverse characters and heart racing action. Do not sleep on this debut!

— JASMINE WATSON, AUTHOR OF TORN

A spellbinding love letter to both fantasy and inclusivity, truly one of a kind.

— CHAR , @CHARSREADINGCORNER

A truly lovely expression of the tenderness of friendship and the lengths one goes to protect the people they love

— CELINE, @BOOKISHWITHB

Libby,
Thank you so much for the support!

A TEMPEST OF EMERALD DREAM

WILLIAM J WOOD

Happy reading! :)

williamjwoodauthor.com

To the short chapter lovers, you're sexy

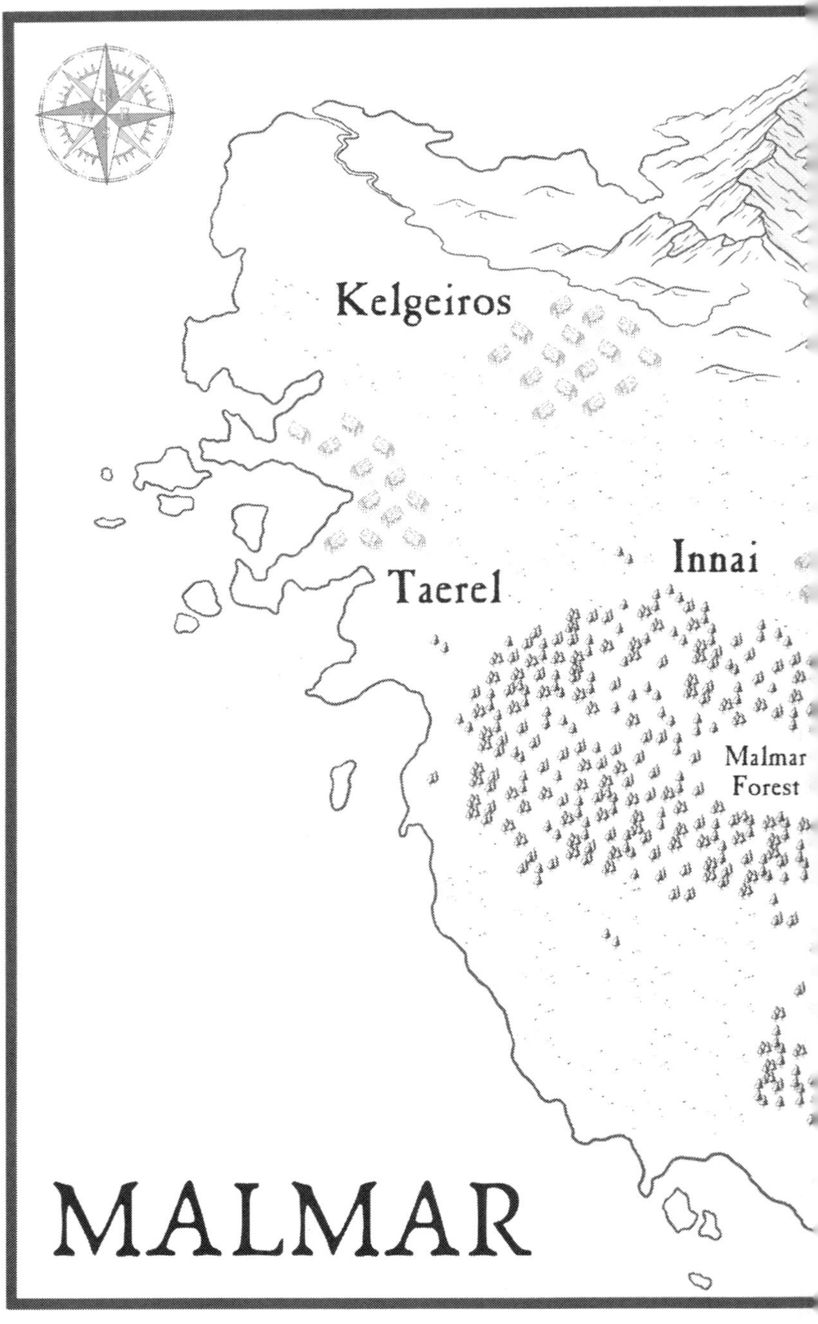
Kelgeiros
Innai
Taerel
Malmar
Forest
MALMAR

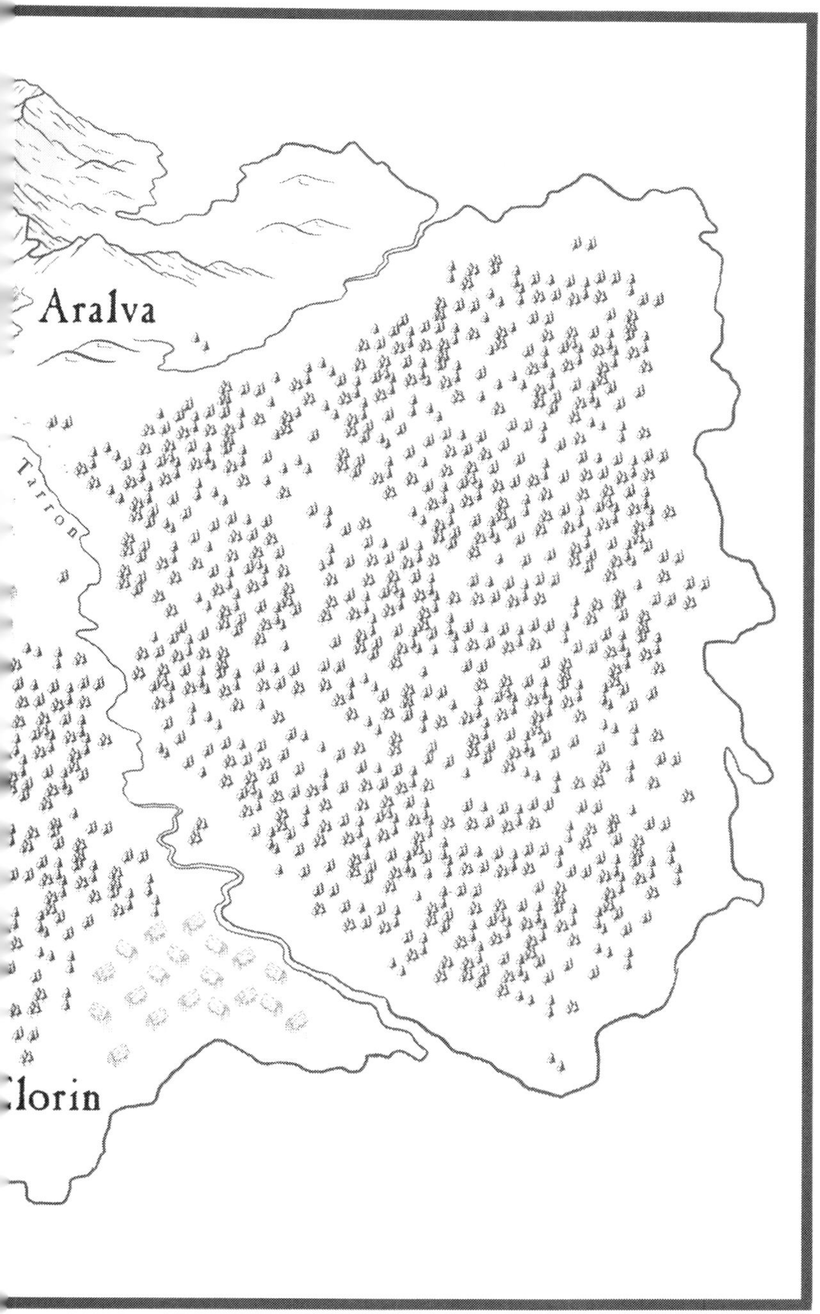
Aralva
Tarron
Clorin

Feather and thorn. Two constants that never intertwine, until now.

— AYEN MORGWYN

CHAPTER 1

By the heart of the nexus, Alleria shed the past and welcomed the new, only to be destroyed by the familiar. Ancient lands bled a rich emerald green. The blow fractured the hope. And the nexus itself. She quickly dodged the next one, but blood brought flame—

"Alleria, can you please put the book down and help me?" A voice boomed from the other side of the room. Mother. It wasn't hard to distinguish, considering she was the only other soul in the house. Only them… forever. She shot from her seat, not before placing her bookmark between the pages of the book she was currently reading. Having just arrived in the library, new books were rare in Elorin, and she couldn't lose the opportunity to snag a quick glance. As a librarian for four years, she had only seen a handful of stock that wasn't older than the town itself. But she loved her job. Spending all day reading when there were no customers felt less like work and more like leisure. It was her chance to escape from her mother's often controlling hold on her. She knew she meant it with love, but it overwhelmed her.

"Coming," Alleria replied, mimicking her mother's strident tone. When she rounded the corner, mistakes were made. Standing hand on hip and eyebrows raised was none other than Pyria, her mother. Her red hair sat gracefully on top of her head, perfectly complimenting her ruby dress. She parted her lips, most likely to scold Alleria's attitude, but Alleria would not give her the chance.

"What is it, Mother?" Alleria continued softly, smiling as if her life depended on it. She crossed her left leg behind her right.

Rolling her eyes, Pyria picked up something from the table. A letter, sealed with red wax. She never wrote letters. Weird. "I just wanted to ask if you would deliver this to Tanyth on the way to the library." Tanyth, her best friend. He had run Elorin's lumber mill since the passing of his father a few years back. She didn't know how he did it. It was enough trouble organizing library books, let alone chopping and collecting wood. But he had always done it. When Alleria and Aiwen, her other best friend, went hunting, he could never come. Always too busy.

"Definitely," she said, taking the letter from Pyria. "What is it?"

"An order for some wood."

Alleria eyed her conspicuously. "What need could you possibly have for wood?" Her mother wasn't overtly crafty.

Pyria scoffed. "For your information, I wish to make some planters for the garden."

It was unruly out there. Her mother never really bothered with the garden until a few weeks ago when her friend remarried following the passing of her husband. She didn't act any differently, but Alleria could tell she wasn't ok. The fake smiles. Her put on happiness. But the garden became her serenity.

Tanyth's house was quaint. And almost withering. When she knocked on the door, it threatened to collapse beneath the pressure. But it didn't. It held, albeit only just. Rustling and heavy steps sounded from inside. More than two feet, it sounded. Eventually, the door rocked open. Tanyth's shirt flung on but his hair was still somehow perfect.

"Al, you ok?" He asked. The door was ajar like he was blocking her from peering inside. She tried, but his large frame did not allow her to see much. His hours carrying lumber had its benefits, it seemed. His quizzical face rested when his fluttering eyes noticed the letter in her hands. "From your mother?"

Quick to grab the letter when she raised it up, "Yes," she said at last.

"I'll get this in right away, it should be ready for her tomorrow."

"Great," she replied. It didn't seem he was in the mood for a conversation. She didn't have the time anyway. "Well, I have to get to work. I'll see you later?"

"Definitely. Bye Al." Already closing the door as he spoke, Alleria sensed he was hiding something. Sneaking a look into the window as she walked past just to confirm her suspicions, she knew it. A familiar face was pressed against Tanyth's lips. Aiwen.

As soon as she stepped into the library, a bitter wind and a sense of dread washed over her. A sinking feeling, so familiar. But so far away. She glanced behind the towering shelves to the rows of gilded windows. The sun glared through the stained glass. Her brows stretched upward, confusion glazing her senses. It was glorious outside; it made no sense. She closed the door behind her and walked headfirst into her trepidation.

CHAPTER 2

A frigid wind blew harsh upon the back of Alleria Valrona, causing her body to arch and her teeth to chatter. Rigorous tremors shot through her frame, so much so, she lost grip of the quill between her pale fingers. The aged tan feather did not float, nor did it fall to the oak table below. Instead, just as she tried to grab it, another gust crashed around her body, carrying the quill in tow before dropping it to the hard floor. Before another unsought gale could disturb her writing, Alleria rose from her seat and craned her neck to deduce the origin of the icy draught. Rows of arched windows, tinted with every colour under the sun, graced the library's north sector. All shut but one.

Pushing the antique chair backward, Alleria

hobbled to close the window. With every stride Alleria took, the temperature plunged. She hugged herself to conserve heat, but it was no use. Her body stiffened, and she watched in terror as ice invaded her surroundings. Deathly icicles seeped through the ceiling, augmenting in front of Alleria's eyes, before hurdling to the ground. In a matter of moments, the library was in spoils, ravaged by the ice. The stained windows, now dressed in fractals of glacial blue, hissing and screaming— The windows shattered inward.

A medley of glass and ice barrelled toward her, so interlaced she could not tell the difference. Before the assault of deathly shards pierced her pale skin, a blast of wintry air struck her, discharging her from the icy prison. But her lips were frozen in place and no one could hear her screams. She just hoped someone might smell the overwhelming smell of petrichor in the air.

Her body flew with the grace of a bird with a clipped wing. Forcing her eyes shut, she shielded the bitter winds and her imminent fate. She did not see the ground getting closer or feel the pain when her body hit the stone floor.

Only darkness.

• • •

VALLEYS OF GREEN ENVELOPED ALLERIA'S VISION. Eyes watering at the beauty that encased her. She did not suppress her awe as she stumbled backward. A myriad of flowers dusted her viridescent surroundings, creating a harmony of colour. The terrain was so vivid, so beautiful.

She spun, her gaze flashing rapidly, glorying in the allure of nature. The soaring valleys seemed to obscure, and ahead a sizeable village lay. The tip of a clock tower protruded from the stone walls. It was grand and evidently aged but displayed no time. Intrigued, Alleria stepped forward, her eyes still fixated on the towering construction. The clock had no hands. *How peculiar*. Alleria let her gaze drift away from the odd sight, stalling mere lengths away from the village gate. Surely, she had not wandered that far. She saw signs surrounded the gates, but only one seized her attention.

Welcome to Aralva.

Alleria rubbed her eyes, making sure she had read the wooden sign correctly. "Welcome to Aralva," she said, trepidation seeping from the words. From when she was just a child, she was told stories of a land far away. A place of light and hope. A home to creatures she could not even imagine. But they were fables.

Taking a reluctant breath, Alleria sealed her

eyes and took a step. And another. When her lids finally fluttered open, she was over Aralva's boundaries. Bustling crowds, not unlike the ones in her home village, encompassed her. Then she saw the pointed ears. And horns. Creatures of stories and myths, inundated her. She struggled not to gasp, but a negligible sound escaped her rosy lips. So enamoured, she almost didn't feel the sudden pressure on her shoulder. A hand. Jutting her head around, she met a vacant face. A face without features, only indents where they should be. She opened her mouth to scream, but no sound came.

"Find us," the faceless figure croaked.

DAWN STREAMED IN FROM EVERY DIRECTION. Opening her eyes, Alleria spotted her belongings. She was in her bedroom. A simple room, but still homely. But what of the library? Her haven. Her safe space. It could not be destroyed. Suddenly, a presence on either side of her made itself known. She knew who they were before they even spoke.

"You're awake!" A loud voice said. Tanyth.

"You worried us there, Al." Aiwen laughed.

Alleria let her eyes float to each boy. They certainly looked better than she felt. Without even looking down, she could feel the bruises that plastered her body. The pain was a dull ache, more annoying than agonising. "What happened?" she asked.

"Freak storm!" Aiwen said. "It seems like it only reached the library… Wrong place, wrong time… How are you feeling?"

"I have felt better," she replied. The figure from her dreams still occupied every one of her thoughts. Why did she need to find them? And who? Why did the dream feel so real? "How damaged is the library?"

"It has seen better days."

"Is everything ruined?"

"Relax," he said. "There are things that survived. Not many books… but some. Although, that doesn't matter unless you're ok."

The books. *Her books*. They were her life. "I need to go look." Alleria lifted her head from the pillow and contorted her frame until her legs dangled from the bed. Pain charged through her being, but she thrusted her legs on the ground, bruises and cuts did indeed cover them. Tugging at her nightdress, she attempted to conceal the wounds.

"Stop, Alleria." Tanyth said, standing in front of her. Tanyth was always the fun and sarcastic friend. She knew him his whole life. This was unlike him. It was the sternest she had ever seen him. "You need to rest." His hand nuzzled her back down as she took to her feet.

"I just need to see it."

"Why?"

"I just *need* to." Alleria snapped.

Tanyth's eyes widened, and Aiwen giggled under his breath. "Al, what is wrong?"

"Nothing, it was just a rotten dream."

"It was more than just a nightmare, Al. You were in a freak storm. Not many people can say that. Being scared is natural." Aiwen now squatted on the bed. He spoke in a lower tone. Serious. "Besides, you look awful. If I didn't know better, I would've thought one of the bears had got to you... you *need* to rest." Aiwen now squatted on the bed. His hazel eyes oozed with concern, perfectly complimenting his dark skin and soft features. Despite his preferences, and their friendship, she nevertheless recognised his good looks.

"I am not scared. I—" Alleria stopped herself.

"Go on," the boys said in unison. Aiwen and Tanyth sat side by side on the bed, their eyes concentrated upon Alleria. She surrendered a hefty sigh, signalling defeat, and gave in to her friend's persistence.

"Do you remember the tales of Aralva?"

• • •

ALLERIA DID NOT BRUSH OVER ANY DETAIL OF HER dream. The two men did not mutter a word until she was done. After decades together, they knew not to interrupt Alleria when she told a story. Aiwen's hand rested on Tanyth's, not in fear but in intrigue. When Alleria noticed, they jutted apart. She drew a curious smile at their shyness and wound up the story. She rested her hands in her lap and let the weight of it all slip off her shoulders.

Aiwen interrupted the blanket of silence. "Do you think the storm in the library was connected to your nightmare?"

Alleria broaden her eyes at her friend's query. Her mouth went dry.. "You actually believe me?"

"Al, you are a nutter, but you're not stupid. And besides, it cannot be a coincidence that you had this dream only moments after a snowstorm *attacked* you and nobody else."

"Ice," Alleria said, her lip quivering into a grin. Aiwen reached forward and nudged her shoulder, snickering. She had to lighten the mood somehow.

"I'm with Aiwen here," Tanyth said. His soft golden curls bounced as he spoke, almost like they were crafted by the Light itself. Tanyth's features were also soft, but unlike Aiwen, his were offset by thick arched brows, much darker than the head on his hair with a deathly sharp jawline. "Promise to rest tonight, and we will all go to the library tomorrow."

Aiwen arched his brow and craned his neck to his friend. "We will?"

"Yes, we will," Tanyth said, eyeing Aiwen firmly. He took Alleria's hands in his and gripped them tight. The heat sent a shiver through her body, reminding her of the storm. Yet, this shiver was welcomed. It made her feel protected. "Deal?" He held still as he awaited her answer, biting his lip with cautious hope.

"Deal."

"Good, we will be back tomorrow morning." Aiwen said. The boys now stood, adjusting their tunics and attempting to alleviate the creases from the woven fabric. Alleria's story had lasted hours. Lounging in their work attire was not a great idea. "If you need me, I'll be at Tan- I'll be at home."

Immediately, Aiwen's face brightened to a vivid ruby flame. Alleria parted her mouth to speak, but he was already out the door. Tanyth shot a flash of a crooked smile her way and followed, blinking rapidly. She just watched as he bumped into the adjacent wall on the way out and eventually shut the door behind him.

She traced the cracks in the wooden frame,

simpering to herself at her friend's poor acting skills. For months, they had been involved. Alleria knew it. However, she would never interfere. She respected her friends too much. They would tell her when they were ready. Until then, Alleria closed her eyes, hoping she would dream of Aralva again. Of the glory, beauty, and culture for her to explore. She jutted in and out of slumber, fearing the ice would return, until finally succumbing to the tender and alluring seductress of sleep.

CHAPTER 3

The faceless figure loomed in front of her. She didn't know how to react. Silence suffocated her as a surge of unrelenting fear crashed inside her being. Finally, she let her eyes stray away from the nightmare fuelled face and to her arms. Her skin had turn pallid in fear. From the corner of her eye, long blond hair spilled from the individual's head, a luscious sleek wave only breached by pointed ears that cut through like a knife.

An elf.

All she knew of elves were from her mother's stories. Some were able warriors and archers. Some possessed the elements. Elves did not attune to one gender; they were fluid. Free. But her mother did not acknowledge them as faceless

—not that she could recall. But it *had* been a long while since her mother told her stories.

Alleria could not deal with the shrilling silence. She spoke. "Who are you?"

"Find us, Alleria Valrona," the elf said gravelly.

"How do you know my name?" Alleria stepped back, trying to broaden the gap between herself and the elf. Her knees threatened to buckle beneath her. But at her second step, their gaze shot toward her feet, paralysing her. How—

"You are not to fear me, young one," the nameless elf said, stepping forward. "Find us."

"Why?" Alleria said, her eyebrows arched.

"Find us, Alleria Valrona, for the mountain's hold is lapsing. Darkness already escaped its clutch, and we foresee it is only a matter of time before Tejon is no more."

Despite their absence of features, Alleria noticed the fear, the consternation in the elf's tone.

"What mountain?" Unbeknownst to what the elf spoke about, Alleria continued to ask questions. What could she do to help? "I am just a librarian. I do not know this Tejon you speak of."

"Very well, child." The elf raised a hand before dropping it again in a diving motion. With that, another valley appeared outside Aralva, a veil unravelled. That is when she realised it was not a valley at all. It was a mountain. It towered over Aralva, and suddenly Alleria felt tiny. The peak of Tejon was hundreds of metres high; taller than anything she'd seen in her life. She had to slap a hand over her mouth to silence her petrified gasps. It made her realise how little of the world she had seen. How small she was in the bigger scheme of things. Elorin was an ounce of what Malmar had to offer.

"For millennia, the elves of Aralva and the whole of Malmar have concealed and protected Mount Tejon. A time ago, an unspeakable evil rained hellfire on these very lands. She— it wiped out many lives until the Elven armies trapped the evil inside Mount Tejon. Many elves died that day, and our numbers have never recovered. But even now, we guard Tejon."

The elf tightened their lip as if the words were hard to speak, even after all this time. She noticed their lip tremble for a brief second. "That was, until a few days ago. A rumble cracked the earth, and darkness escaped the mountain's grasp. Only an essence of the evil broke free. It is only a matter of time before Tejon is no more. Alleria, you must find us, for you are our sole hope."

"Why me?" Alleria blurted. "I promise, I am

of no use to you-" Alleria stopped, realising she still did not know the name of the elf that stood before her. "Who are you?"

"My name is Ayen Morgwyn." Like magic, the guise upon the elf's face dissolved, and golden shining eyes peered back at her. Every feature on their face was sharp. Their cheekbones were so clean cut, the bones almost pierced through skin. A face she had never seen before. Ayen's mouth parted, as did Alleria's at the spectacle that transpired.

Ayen spoke, his voice heightened, clearly astonished that Alleria could see their face. "An age-old Elven magic protects an elf's identity from birth. Only when someone learns of their name and bears the elf's permission does the magic fade. I did not allow you to see my face, Alleria. Is that proof enough? You *are* different. Our saviour."

How could Alleria respond to that? Her mind reeled. Was this real? A mere fragment of her wild imagination? Her brows drew closer. "Well, Ayen. Sorry to say, but this is surely a mistake. I am a librarian, a curator, if you will. I genuinely think I am just having another awful vivid dream."

"I wish this was but a dream, child. However, no one is purely one thing in life. My ancestors built Elven ideologies on fluidity and choice. Yes, you may be what you wish. You choose to be an artisan of books and language. Child, prophecies are bound. And you, Alleria, are foretold to conquer the darkness. Alleria Valrona, you are our saviour. Here." Ayen took Alleria's hand in theirs. Alleria, to her own surprise, let them. Their finger flexed in the bright Malmar sun before lowering to Alleria's palm and scratching it.

Alleria winced at the short, but acute twinge and stared as a thin line of red oozed from her hand.

"When you wake from this *dream,* you will realise this is very real."

She nodded, but from their speech, only one thing recurred in her head. "What prophecy?" Alleria asked. She crossed her arms, offering a nonchalant impression. But that was far from the truth. It intrigued Alleria. Was this why her mother told her so many stories of Aralva?

"The elves of the past foretold, since the emergence of Elven history, that in her twentieth year, the saviour will eradicate the evil for good. It is clear your powers manifested to some extent. Otherwise, you would still be in Elorin."

"I just don't understand. I was in the library, and it was cold. There was ice and—"

"As I said, your powers have manifested. I did not summon you here. Your power is calling you to us. I simply answered the call. Learn to control your gift, Alleria. Find us. Find us soon."

Alleria was dumbstruck. A sudden feeling of heaviness blossomed inside her. She generated the storm in the library? She nearly killed *herself*? How does that make sense? After what seemed like an age, she murmured, "What is its name?"

"Whose name?"

"The evil," Alleria said anxiously.

THEY SWALLOWED HARD.

"Its name is Naesaela."

❄

THE LIBRARY WAS WORSE THAN SHE HOPED IT WOULD be. Hundreds of books cluttered the floor, requiring her and the lads to hop through the hallways. She needed to locate a book about Aralva. She knew it was not a dream anymore—the faint laceration on her hand affirmed that conjecture. Scabbing already, it wasn't there when she fell asleep. When she woke, she updated Aiwen and Tanyth on everything: Ayen, the prophecy, and *Naesaela*. They simply nodded as she told the story of her *dream* and vowed to help her find out what they could. She had never known them to be so helpful. But she hoped they weren't helping her out of the guilt of their relationship.

"Here!" Aiwen said, his voice distant behind an overturned bookcase. "I think it's the only tome that wasn't destroyed to some extent." He held up an aged book that had somehow withstood the polar storm only days ago. In fact, as Alleria held its leather casing in her hands, she realized it was in perfect condition. Yes, aged like most books, but perfectly intact. Was it preserved by a similar Elven magic to Tejon? If so, she would not be surprised, not after what she witnessed in her dreams.

The History of Malmar bared across the front of the tome in a mysterious red ink. *Surely not blood,* she thought as she gyrated her hair between her fingers. The book was bulky and called for two hands to open. Luckily, she had help as she was still shaky. She settled it on the floor, sweeping debris away. Aiwen and Tanyth held each side of the book open. They gawked at the blank page, lifting every worn page. Yet no text bared on any of them. Completely empty.

. . .

"I don't understand," Alleria said, wanting to claw her tired hands at the pages. She struggled to disguise the frustration in her voice. She did not want her friends to see her low. She never did. Alleria was the *stable* one. "The only book in this entire library that lasted the storm, and it is devoid of anything. Surely, we must be missing something." Alleria slumped back, resting her back on an fallen shelf and dropped her head. Tanyth and Aiwen looked at each other, their eyes glazed with worry. Then Aiwen's pupils turned hopeful.

"You say this *Ayen* told you that *you* conceived the storm?"

"Yes."

"Well, why don't you try to funnel that *power* into the book. Magic shrouded the elf's face. Who is to say the book isn't too? If it truly holds the exact whereabouts of Aralva, it will not be easy to find. Right?"

Alleria's eyes lit up before dimming again before the boy's eyes. "Aiwen, you are a genius! But I do not know if I can recreate *that* power again."

"You will never know if you do not try, Alleria," he said, his palms settling on the open book, wheedling her. Nervously, Alleria's eyes shifted between the book and the boys. Indeed, an attempt would hurt nobody. Sweat beaded her upper lip as she stooped forward. The last time she used her *power*, she almost killed herself. And she hadn't even realised she was controlling it. What even was her ability? How did it work?

"I would just like to remind you both how unstable this building is. We probably shouldn't even be in here," Tanyth said. "We should hurry matters up a little." Alleria tried not to chuckle at his panicked statement, but she could not help but release a faint snicker. Normally, Tanyth would never willingly show his fear.

AFTER A MOMENT, ALLERIA DREW A DEEP BREATH and, on the exhale, placed her palms on the book. Closing her eyes, she thought of Aralva. The valleys. Ayen. Heat emanated from her palms. So much so, Aiwen and Tanyth pulled their own from the book. They threw their gazes to Alleria for reassurance. Her eyes were closed but somehow sensed their stares and nodded. What was this *magic*?

The boys stumbled back, observing as the hot and cool air intertwined and blurred their surroundings. Heat shot back into the pages, the world suddenly in reverse. Alleria opened her eyes, and the tome sealed with a loud bang.

Tanyth shuffled forward to reclaim his original space, but she gestured him to remain where he was. Silence shook the library for what felt like minutes until Alleria said. "Aralva."

In a blink, the book flew open, and light erupted from its pages, shooting skyward like a beacon. The boys watched in bewilderment. Alleria was not insane. She had power. Real power. Aralva was real.

The light show lasted only a few moments, but it could have lasted hours for all they knew. When it subsided, Alleria slumped back to the bookcase and groaned. "I think it is done."

Tanyth and Aiwen eyed each other before inching forward. The book remained open. Colour and text littered the pages. Tanyth felt the goosebumps form on his arms when he picked up the book, which rapidly withdrew with the lingering heat dancing through his bones. "Alleria, you did it," Tanyth said as he laughed through his teeth. "You are unbelievable." His eyes veered to where she slumped on the floor. Her eyes were open, but her pupils were black.

Aiwen was soon at her side, lightly shaking her awake. He placed his trembling finger on her neck to locate a steady pulse. A heavy sigh left his lips. "She just blacked out," he said, planting his hand on his chest to feel his own heartbeat.

Tanyth did the same before mopping the perspiration from his brow—he could not tell if the heat or the panic of the situation were to blame. "It was a lot of power. I'm amazed she didn't pass out sooner."

A FOREIGN VOICE CUT THROUGH LIKE A KNIFE. "SHE has always been a strong one."

CHAPTER 4

"You knew this whole time?" Alleria asked, now awake but, once again, bound to her bed. Anger seethed in her words and she did not hold back. Her pulse was racing. With dishevelled flaming hair loosely thrusted into a bun on her head, her mother, Pyria, rounded the bed before setting her slim frame on an armchair. Pyria stared back at her, anguish behind her eyes but sternness in her jaw, hanging her head low. She did not make any eye contact as she spoke.

"You were born in Aralva—" She did not look up as she spoke. Her eyebrows just gathered in, a pained expression plastered on her face.

"What?" Alleria interjected, her eyes practically leaping from their sockets. Her mother smoothed her hand to appease her.

"Please let me explain." Taking a profound breath before proceeding, her mother smoothed her hand to appease her. "You were born in Aralva, the village past where the river splits. I hear from Tanyth and Aiwen that you know of it already, so I shall skip that part. When you were born, the earth rumbled, signalling the emergence of the saviour. We never expected it to be you." She stifled back a cry. "No one could have guessed."

DESPITE HER RESENTMENT, ALLERIA SQUEEZED HER mother's hand. She was close to leaving the room, but a mother's love is sometimes irresistible. Pyria looked into her eyes with a faintly pained smile carved on her lips. Her face shone slightly and she leaned just a little closer.

"The council visited us that day. Instructing us that the guards would come that evening to take you away and train you into the saviour they wished you to be. Your Father and I were selfish. How can someone subject an infant to something so dangerous at such an inexperienced age." Her voice became intense now. "So we deserted. That night, the guards encountered empty beds. We were deep into the forests by the time they discovered us gone, but, somehow, they still found us. Your father held them at bay so we could escape. They took him and tried him for treachery. Executed three days later."

Alleria's head revolved at the prospect of it. *She* murdered her father, all because *she* was the saviour. Something she herself could not believe. Her mother had only been trying to protect her. But how could Alleria forgive her for suppressing an entire part of her life from her? Her father saved them. But at what cost.

Her power.

Her destiny.

"How do you know Father died?" Alleria asked, working to shelter the tremors in her voice. She laid a hand against her chest and resisted the urge to ball her shirt into a fist.

"Marriage in Aralva is sacred. Through Elven magic, you are linked. On the third day of our escape, I felt the tie snap." Pyria wiped the last of her tears with the back of her sleeve and surrendered her auburn hair from the ties on her head. Brushing her hands through it, She dispelled the tangles.

"You should have told me," Alleria said. "I deserved to know."

"I didn't want to see my baby sent away to sacrifice herself. I should have given you that choice. I'm sorry."

Alleria nodded but her mind told a different story. She didn't know what to think. Who to trust. This could all be another lie—she wouldn't put it past her now.

Lethargy filled her veins. Feeling empty, she sought to lift her head from the bed, but it would not move. Even batting her eyelids became a chore. For a moment, the two sat in silence before Alleria muttered. "I'm going to go to Aralva."

Her mother leaned back in the chair. "If that is your choice, then I respect it." Pyria forced a smile. It was obvious she didn't want her to. But she couldn't stop her. Not now. Not after all the deceit.

The door screeched open, and her friends peeked their heads in.

"May we enter?" Aiwen asked.

"Of course," Pyria said. Her face loosened and the boys tumbled in. Her mother rose from her seated position, lightly dropping Alleria's hand as she did so, and strode for the door. "Please, do not take off without saying goodbye," was all she said before closing the door behind her.

"Did you hear all of that?" Alleria asked, cringing at the thought. She was uncertain why, but she had always been the *normal* person. No family melodrama, except the unknown passing of her father when she was young. She knew nothing of the details. Now the truth had come to light. Her father had not died. He was murdered.

TANYTH SHOT HER A CROOKED SMILE. "WE DID."

"Great."

"If it makes you feel any better, we brought this." Tanyth pulled something from behind his back. The book. Alleria jumped forward, neglecting how weak she was, and sank back to the cushioned surface below. With a heavy stomach, she sighed. She wasn't used to feeling so… weak. So powerless.

"Calm ye reins, horsey." Aiwen said. Alleria glared at him with eyes of smouldering frenzy. Watching as his pupils dilated in regret, she let him suffer for a moment more before chuckling.

"Take a joke," she said, nudging him. "You deserve a taste of your own medicine." Aiwen stood straight, trying to hide his reddening cheeks and his quivering chin.

"I cannot hold this book all night," Tanyth said. With that, he dropped the tome to the bed, just beneath Alleria's feet. The heft of it almost collapsed the frame. With the little strength she had, Alleria hauled closer. As her fingers traced the cover's typography, she could feel the remnants of energy. Power trapped in the pages.

• • •

ARALVA FLASHED IN HER MIND. THE BUSTLING streets and creatures she never believed to have existed just two nights ago. Her thoughts turned sour when she remembered the council, the ones responsible for her father's death. She did not know how she'd react if she saw them in the flesh, and she did not want to know. For she could only assume her emotions controlled her power somehow. Finally, she thought of Ayen and hoped they had nothing to do with their barbaric schemes and actions.

The book creaked as Alleria opened it and cracked the spine. The pages bore ink of every colour under the sun, shades she had never seen in Elorin before. Before Alleria could give it another thought, the pages came alive. Moving like a feather in the wind, elegantly but with urgency. It settled on a map, only a few pages from the back of the tome. The cartography, unlike the rest of the book, looked old, labelling some of the surrounding villages by their previous names. By this point, the boys were at either side of Alleria, their eyes fixated on the frayed pages. The three gazed attentively, studying for any sign of Aralva, but there was nothing.

"I do not see Aralva," Alleria said, quieter than she expected. She almost groaned, but her words were interrupted.

"Wait, look there." Tanyth's finger shot into an unmarked part of the map. It was seemingly left out of the map, a cloud of mist protecting it. His finger grazed the page and fell upon River Tarron. "If you pass through the forest and follow the river north, it eventually splits in two. The unmarked part of the map is between the split—"

"And that is where Aralva lies," Alleria finished. "Tan, you're a genius!" Despite her fragile frame, she broke to her right and planted a kiss on his cheek. He blushed and looked to Aiwen for reassurance, but he only laughed and stuck his thumbs up.

"We're really doing this?" Aiwen asked, bringing the reality of the situation back to the three. It was a treacherous journey, five days with horseback at least.

Alleria's gaze sank to her lap and then to her friends.

"I'm not expecting either of you to want to do this. But I have to."

"We're coming," the boys said in unison without a word of apprehension. She knew all they wanted was one thing, Her safety. They could not let her travel so far by herself. Yes, she could handle a bow and arrow better than most. But if Ayen was forthright about the evil that escaped the mountain, it was only a matter of time before they witnessed it for themselves.

Alleria smiled widely, bundling her arms around them both. "If you change your mind, I promise I won't bite."

"We've heard that before." Aiwen said. "When do we leave?"

Tanyth shifted in his seat, awaiting Alleria's answer. She needed time to rest, but time is what they didn't have. The whole of Malmar depended on her.

"At first light."

THEY PLOTTED THEIR TRAVELS THROUGH THE NIGHT, and only when the clock struck midnight did they rest. When the boys left for their homes, Alleria struggled to stop her head from reeling. Just two days ago, she was the quiet, innocent town librarian. She loved working with books every day, serving her fellow villagers, and reading in her off time. Novels of enigma and mystery were her preferred read, but now her life was a mystery. She was a living story. In the future, people would write about *her.*

Her life was upside down. Her mother had

lied to her for her whole life, about where she was from and about her father. She didn't know *how* to feel about it. She didn't want to be angry with her mother but she couldn't just pretend like it never happened. Her mother might have cost Malmar everything.

Trying to distract herself, Alleria shuffled beneath her bedding and shifted her focus to the plan. She forgot to ask Aiwen and Tanyth about the horses they required for their journey. Alleria's mother owned a horse, but the boys did not. *We'll have to make do,* she thought as her eyes finally shut for the night.

CHAPTER 5

A blood-curdling scream awoke Alleria with a startle. Sweat beaded on her forehead. No sunlight, just rich darkness. But as Alleria peered through her draperies, it wasn't night, nor was it day. Clouds of black littered the sky, thwarting any semblance of time. A pang of confusion clouded her. Only the Light knew if she had slept through first light. Her bedroom door swung open, and Pyria stood with an exasperated expression on her face. She wailed her name and embraced her intently. After a few moments, Alleria broke from the hug.

"What is going on?" she said, panic radiating in her tone and firing a quizzing glance at her mother. She didn't know how many more unexpected situations she could handle.

"It seems this darkness you spoke of has reached Elorin. The townspeople aren't themselves. They—"

The glass shattered all around them as a rock crashed into the chamber.

"They're here. We need to go," Pyria said, shouting over the noise. "NOW!" Grabbing Alleria's hand, Pyria pulled her daughter through the house, only stopping when they reached the back door. Alleria winced as glass pushed into the soles of her feet, but she did not scream. They had to keep a low profile. As Pyria stuck her head out, she let out a relieved sigh and opened the door fully. Aiwen and Tanyth stood, their clothes dishevelled and ripped.

"I would make a joke if we weren't about to die," Alleria said through her teeth, trying not to yell as she pulled shards of glass from her feet. At the last piece, she rubbed her feet with a sodden rag and placed her shoes on. They were worn and probably would not last the entire journey, but they were all she had. Alleria noted her mother's glowering eyes, but she couldn't help her. They had to leave right away.

"Alleria, we will take Blanchy," her mother said, pointing to the white mare just outside the house. Abruptly, she rounded on the boys. "Go to the stables. Take any horse you can find. We will meet you outside the town gates." The boys bowed and retreated into the gloom of night.

"You're coming with us? But if- when we make it to Aralva, won't the council arrest you on sight?" Alleria said. This wasn't the plan. Her mother was supposed to stay in Elorin, safe. Her mother had lied, but she didn't want to see her dead.

Pyria smiled gently. She had already decided.

"I would rather make certain you are safe and deal with the repercussions afterward." Alleria tried to revolt but was met with another embrace. "Now, come on. Before they find us."

"What happened to the town?"

"The darkness has woven into their minds, changed how they are and how they act," Pyria said, reaching for the bow and quiver that dangled by the door. Her mother placed the quiver on Alleria's back and handed over the bow. Alleria nodded in thanks. "In my youth, I was told legends about how Naesaela could influence one's mind to do its bidding. But now we know, they weren't just legends."

ALLERIA AND HER MOTHER HURRIED THROUGH SIDE streets, sticking to grassy patches whenever they could. Blanchy's hooves didn't make so much commotion in the dirt. They rounded corner after corner, luckily not running into any townspeople. When they approached the top of the street, Pyria jumped from the horse and peered around. Alleria stumbled from the horse and did the same. Hundreds of people lined the main square, impeding any chance of reaching the front gates.

"What are we going to do?" Alleria asked, almost forgetting to be as silent as possible. Pyria looked at her daughter, then to the tainted towns' peoples. Her gaze floated for a moment, concentrating and angling back to Alleria. She already knew what her mother was going to suggest.

"I'm going to divert them," Pyria said.

Pain washed over Alleria's eyes. "No—"

"Let me finish. I'm going to distract them. It will give you the best chance to get out of here. When you are outside the gates, wait a few moments for the boys. However, if they are not there, you must get out."

"Mother, no!"

Pyria jumped out into the open and shrieked. Instantly, the possessed townspeople wailed themselves and tracked her mother through the side streets.

. . .

SHE WANTED TO RUN AFTER HER, BUT IT WOULD BE reckless. Instead, Alleria let out a whimper and mounted Blanchy, dashing through the square and out of the Elorin gates. Nothing was right. She was alone. The only disturbance now, the muffled yells now seemingly far away. Pulling the reins lightly, Blanchy halted, and Alleria waited. *Please, do not make me do this alone,* she pleaded internally, clenching her chest. She could not lose everyone she loved tonight. Hooves shattered through the muted bellows at that moment, and Aiwen and Tanyth appeared seated on a black and white stallion, respectively. Alleria noticed smiles lurched on their faces as they came closer until they noticed Pyria's absence.

"WHERE IS PYRIA?" TANYTH ASKED AS HIS HORSE settled beside Alleria.

"She broke off to distract them. I tried to stop her—"

"This isn't your fault," Aiwen said, pulling his horse to other side. The boys always seemed to be near when she called for someone. "We cannot stop. We need to create some distance."

Alleria nodded. As she turned Blanchy to face north, something stopped her— Her mother screaming her name. Pyria ran through the square, hundreds of townspeople on her back. Like a trail of fire, her auburn hair gracefully flowed behind her. Her long skirt was slashed up the side, easing the drag as she ran.

"MOTHER!" SHE CALLED OUT, TWISTING THE HORSE to the village once again. She heard one of the boys mutter, 'be careful,' but she had to save her mother. She didn't want to think about what would happen if she didn't. Her mother's eyes lit up, reaching the gate. She had done it. Her heroic gesture allowed them to escape. Mere metres away, Pyria reached for Alleria's hand.

Blood splattered everywhere.

Before Alleria could scream, Aiwen hauled her away. She felt him tug at the Blanchy's reins, and the horse shot into motion. She watched as the people she grew up with trampled her mother. People she served every day in the library. Alleria cried so vehemently, a siren would be taken aback. A warmth festered inside her, craving to escape. So she let it. A flurry of light erratically exploded from Alleria's being. She couldn't command it or hone it in a specific direction. It was everywhere.

. . .

THE ONCE DARKENED SKIES WERE NOW LUMINOUS. IT was not sky blue but rich yellow, like the sun was around them. Alleria jumped from Blanchy's saddle and strode toward her mother. Instinctively, she reached for an arrow, but she didn't need it. Nor would it have helped. Her screams grew, deaf to Aiwen and Tanyth's cries for her to return. She hurled her arms around her mother. The boys watched dumbfoundedly as slices of light shot from her palms into her attackers and beyond. Chaos. Blasts sliced straight through Elorin's gates. Her mother was all she could think about. Believing her power rooted itself in emotion, she was right.

With one ending cry, she thrusted her arms in front of her. A scythe of shimmering light swung through every individual who stood in her path. A purple mist escaped their bodies as they dropped to the floor, finally revealing where her mother lay. Alleria cupped her hands under her mother's head, and let her eyes skim her body. She observed the bruises and cuts that littered Pyria's body. Only a single tear shed.The golden sky soon dwindled to reveal dawn. They didn't miss first light after all. Swinging her mother's lifeless body in her arms, the boys finally caught up with her. Tanyth reached down and placed his fingers on her neck.

"She's still alive," he said. "She's weak, but there is still a pulse." Alleria's eyes lit up in an instant.

"What do we do?" she asked Tanyth, her eyes continually flitting from Pyria to her friend.

"Well, we can't leave her here. I say we take her with us. But, I can't say if she'd survive the journey." His face was straight. Alleria knew he'd been reluctant to disclose any emotion, to avert any more upset.

Alleria nodded. "Are they dead?" She croaked, her gaze only briefly reaching for the bodies that surrounded them. Aiwen walked to a body and reached down.

"They're alive," he said. "Alleria, you didn't kill them. I can only assume you rid their body of the darkness, somehow. It's remarkable, but I don't know how you did it." His hands ran through his hair. Trying to bring him back to reality, Tanyth patted Aiwen's back.

"Can you lift her to Blanchy, please?"

The boys nodded and pulled Pyria from the cold ground before settling her on the horse.

"I'm going to walk for a while. She needs to lie down and rest," she said.

Tanyth was about to protest, but Alleria stopped him. Her arms raised. "Please, I would like to walk."

Defeated, they resumed their places on their steeds.

"Let us go now then. The darkness that once possessed them may be gone. But I don't know for how long."

Alleria nodded. "To the north, we go."

THEY TRUDGED THROUGH BARREN FIELDS FOR HOURS, keeping quiet except for the routine checks on Pyria. Her frame was stiff, and her head hot. Alleria kept to herself, afflicted by her own anxieties. The light that escaped her hands scared her. It hadn't killed anyone, but what if it had? At the threshold of spiralling, Alleria stopped in her tracks. They had finally reached the forest of Malmar. As a child, it was forbidden, for many entered and never returned. But they didn't have a choice. This was quickest route to Aralva. Elorin does reside beside the River Tarron but the rapids in the south of Malmar are deadly. It was not worth the risk. Time was running out, but they were not any use dead.

"Tonight we settle on the forest outskirts," Alleria said, piercing the hours-long silence. "We don't know what lies behind these trees, and I don't want to find out in the dark."

Tanyth and Aiwen didn't respond with

words, just the unloading of bags. Alleria took this time to check on her mother. She watched as her mouth parted every few moments to breathe a bitter breath and a wisp of cold air. The sky had blackened, and the once scorching heat was now but a memory. Alleria pulled a woven blanket her mother had packed from her bag and wrapped it around them both, struggling not to let her incident in the library cloud her thoughts. The chill was a reminder, and she just hoped she wasn't responsible for the weather change.

"Alleria." Her name tore through the air, freeing her from her thoughts. Alleria's head bobbed up from her mother's side to the source of the noise. Tanyth stood beside her, his hand stretched out on her back. Despite the circumstances, his curls still bounced in the increasing moonlight. If only Alleria's hair withstood the changing temperatures, instead, it stuck to her head. But she couldn't tell if it was cold or damp.

"What's wrong?" Alleria finally said, rubbing her tired eyes. His face exuded no emotion, but he couldn't mask the worry that lay behind his eyes.

"Nothing," he was quick to answer in fear of upsetting her more. "But the cold weather, that's not you, is it?" His last words rang with trepidation, expecting to feel the wrath of Alleria's words. But they didn't come.

"I don't think so." Her head fell to her hands. Muffling, she continued "But then again, how am I to know? I didn't know that it was my power in the library. Tanyth." She looked up at her friend, tears in her eyes. "I don't know what I'm doing." Her gaze drifted from his face as she waited for an answer. Aiwen was already asleep. At that moment, Tanyth sat on the floor and tapped the ground beside him. Defeated, Alleria obliged.

"I don't know what is in store for us. The next few weeks will be hell." He took Alleria's chin in his hand and gently twisted her face to his so she could see and believe his words. "But I promise, nothing will happen to any of us. We survived twenty years in Elorin, of all places."

Alleria chuckled at the mention of their village. Food was scarce, and they had to survive. For years, they hunted for their families. Then, at the end of the day, they would share their catches. Some days they wouldn't eat. Others, they'd have enough to feed their families four times over. "Thank you."

"For what?"

"Giving me hope."

CHAPTER 6

Ayen was gone. As were all the inhabitants of Aralva. The once-bustling streets rattled in silence, and the sky was virtually black, like Elorin earlier in the day. The clock tower rang behind her. Without glancing toward it, she pictured its armless face. Yet another mystery that pierced her thoughts. It was then she noticed the valleys. Vibrant green pastures, now grey. She concentrated her gaze and realised it wasn't replaced. It was scorched. Her shoulders tightened at the sight.

The stench of fire and destruction penetrated her senses, and Mount Tejon appeared in front of her. Before it lay dormant, enclosing the evil. But now, evil seeped through the rock and into the world. She watched as black smoke crawled through the mountain turned into something horrifying.

Creatures....

flew everywhere. She tried to speak, but her throat clogged in fear. With every second, they drew near, their calls piercing the once serene landscape. Alleria fell to the floor, closing her eyes and awaiting her death.

A SCREAM TORE FROM ALLERIA'S THROAT, AND SHE shot up. It was but a dream. Aiwen and Tanyth were up in an instant at Alleria's side.

"What happened?" They both said. Trying to comfort her, Tanyth placed a palm on her back. Her heart pounded through her chest. She was no longer cold. Sweat beaded on her forehead, which Aiwen wiped with a cloth.

"Aralva was burning," she finally said, swallowing her fear. "I saw the evil escape from the mountain. I think it was a vision." She fell back onto her makeshift bed and settled on the hard floor. The boys shot each other worried glances and rested beside her.

"WE'RE HERE," TANYTH SAID, WIPING THE WATER from her eyes. "These dreams are *your* power. The same power that saved all those people back in Elorin-"

"The same power that almost killed me," Alleria snapped. She was on her feet in seconds, pacing. "If it wasn't for this *power,* we'd all be safe. And my mother wouldn't be fighting for her life." Her eyes fell to Pyria's resting body. Tanyth had lowered her to the floor before they fell asleep.

"You know that's not true," Aiwen said in defiance. His tone rang with apprehension, but also unbridled rage. "The evil from *that* mountain injured your mother. You *saved* her before they could do more than that." Aiwen looked to Tanyth, afraid he had gone too far. He lifted his hand to apologise, but Alleria halted in place. Her mind raced, searching for an explanation for any of this. But it didn't come. They were in the unknown. And she had to deal with that. For once in her life, she couldn't turn to books for an escape.

"You're right," she eventually said, her head drooped low. "She's all the family I have, so I snapped. I'm taking it out on you, and I'm sorry."

"But that's where you're wrong, Alleria." Tanyth bent toward her. His smile seemed to radiate like the early morning light. "We're your family too. And we're Pyria's."

"Exactly," Aiwen said.

"Thanks for that thoughtful addition, Ai," Tanyth retorted before returning his gaze to Alleria. "Family is what you choose. And we choose you."

In seconds, Alleria was in her friend's arms, cherishing her newfound revelation. Her mind had boggled at the prospect of family after learning her father's fate. But why? Tanyth and Aiwen had been there for their whole life. They were the brothers she never had.

"Thank you," she said. "I understand now. I love you both."

"ALLERIA?" A FAMILIAR VOICE BROKE THROUGH THE commotion. Their heads shot around to find Pyria sitting up. Her face was bruised, but her eyes were bright and well.

"Are you ok?" Alleria said through her cries of glee.

"I'm fine, just a bit sore." She smiled as she felt her ribs, trying to hide the wince of pain. "Where are we?" she finally added, glancing around at her surroundings.

"Right outside the forest. We rested for the night."

"Smart girl."

"Do you think you can stand?"

"I think so."

With that, Pyria clambered to her feet, holding on to Tanyth and Aiwen as she did so. When she stood, the boys let go, and Pyria lost her balance, but she did not fall. Her jaw clenched as she tried to keep upright, her pain apparent.

"I think you should take Blanchy, just until you're stronger on your feet, Mother."

Pyria nodded, wobbling her way to the horse and climbed on, fending off the boys as they tried to help. "I may be crippled, but I will never get better if I do not try for myself first."

"You just woke up, and you want to go already?" Alleria asked.

"The sooner we leave, the sooner this is all done with. Besides, I have been awake for a little while already, Alleria."

"So you heard?"

"I did," Pyria confirmed. She pointed at the boys; their faces widened as she did so. "And they're right. They have been more family to you than I have."

"That's not true—"

"But it is," Pyria interrupted, suddenly losing the prideful tone she was known for. "I lied to you for your whole life. Family is about truth and trust, and I broke that. Alleria, I'm so sorry."

"I know you are, and I'm trying forgive you." Alleria smiled sincerely at her mother. Still unsure, her mother returned the smile but didn't overstep with an embrace. Alleria assumed her mother thought to earn her trust back. Changing the subject, she asked, "Are you sure you can ride already?"

"I have to be. I assume your dreams are getting more… violent."

Alleria nodded.

"Then we must leave now. Naesaela's evil is spreading through Malmar quicker than I thought it would."

HASTILY, AIWEN AND TANYTH PACKED THE BAGS TO avoid the wrath of Pyria. Something they had become all too familiar within the years they'd known Alleria. They always joked she got her *feistiness* from her mother. Mother like daughter.

"What was the *evil's* name again?" Alleria asked.

"Naesaela."

"Why do you say it so easily? The elf from my dream, Ayen, was so hesitant."

"Ah, Ayen. They were a great friend," Pyria said. "It is an Aralvan superstition that saying

Naesaela's name will command you to death. The first of the evil's wrath when it escapes."

"Then why do you say it?"

"Because, Alleria, I have already suffered a fate worse than death." Her lip didn't quiver, and her eyebrows didn't furrow. However, her eyes rang with a melancholy of sorts. *She must* have thought *of father*. "Naesaela does not intimidate me, and I refuse to live my life in fear of a name."

The boys had finished packing their bags and were awaiting further instructions. They slowly guided their steeds towards Alleria and her mother, trying not to disturb their conversation too much. Motioning them to come closer, Alleria smiled before turning back to her mother.

"OK, ARE WE READY?"

"I think so," Tanyth said. He tapped his steed and jumped on it. Aiwen did the same.

"One thing," Pyria said. "Do you have your bow still?"

Alleria felt her back to check and nodded. "Why?"

"Ancient magic guards the forest. Magic, even the elves know little about." She stroked Blanchy's fur as she recounted the story. "When you enter, your power might fail you. So, use your bow if needed."

"I don't think I even want to use my power any time soon after what happened earlier," Alleria retorted. Her mother smiled gently, seemingly wishing she could tell her not to not fear her *gift*. "Does that mean Naesaela's evil will dampen too?"

"One can only hope."

"What do you mean by that?"

Pyria tightened her lip and released a breath. "We are in unknown territory. On paper, the forest's magic *should* stop Naesaela's magic from penetrating the tree-line. But considering it was strong enough to reach Elorin already, now I'm not too sure."

"And if Naesaela's magic reaches the forest, we have no means of defence," Alleria said. Pyria shook her head. Her eyes were bloodshot from the night before, and her hair messier than she would like.

"You must not rely on your magic, Alleria. Yes, it is powerful, but you are much more skilled as an archer. That goes to you too, boys." She turned to Aiwen and Tanyth, who almost jumped at their mention.

"What's that?" Aiwen asked.

"You two are both very skilled as well with your weapons. If needed, use them."

"Of course, Pyria," Tanyth said, reaching behind his back to ensure the cold metal of the axe was still sheathed on his back. He inherited his father's lumber mill when he passed away two years ago and has since become an artisan lumberjack and remarkably proficient with an axe.

"And you?" Pyria turned her attention to Aiwen and eyed the curved mahogany bow that hung from his back. He and Alleria both took up archery at a young age to hunt if the village ever required it.

"Yes, of course," he said. He bit his lip, nervous about the task that awaited them. "I will do everything in my power to keep you all safe." His deep voice oozed in fear, but his words rang true. He would kill if needed. Alleria knew that as much.

When Pyria nodded and looked away, Alleria took Aiwen by his arm and whispered, "I know that look."

"What look?" he said back, in a whispered tone. Crossing his arms, he tried to play nonchalantly and lowered his head.

"We're all nervous—"

"I'm not—"

"I have known you too long to know when you're scared. We're all scared, but we have each other. And family is stronger than anything." Alleria was always the best at uniting the group after an argument or a predicament, and today was no different. Aiwen raised his head to meet Alleria's eye-line.

"Ok," he finally said. "But can we get going? The anticipation is killing me."

Alleria pushed him lovingly. "You can never be serious for a moment, can you?"

"If you *know* me so well," he said as he walked back to Aiwen and Pyria. "You should know the answer to that." He laughed, clearly eased by Alleria's words.

Pyria looked at the boys and then at their steeds. "This is the farthest your horses can go," she said. "They're too big to get through the dense tree-line. Blanchy only just fits."

"Oh," Aiwen said, somewhat embarrassed he hadn't realised earlier, and jumped off. Tanyth did the same and hauled his bag onto his back.

"The Light thanks you for bringing us this far," Tanyth spoke as he patted the mare's side and let it runoff. Aiwen muttered similar words, and they both stared as their mounts disappeared into the early morning light.

Pyria nodded before facing toward the

thicket. She ran her fingers through her auburn hair and said, "Let us go."

THE FOREST WAS NOT ALL DIFFERENT FROM THE woodlands that encompassed Elorin, just more extensive. They had travelled not even five minutes into the wooded area, but no exit was visible. The only light that broke through the tree line hazed everything in a verdant green glow. Alleria would have stopped and marvelled at the terrain if it wasn't for the circumstances.

Her fondness for nature had blossomed when she was young and on the hunt. It was a weird feeling for her. She had such fond memories of those hard times. They ought to have thought she was crazy.

She would return hours after her mother had instructed her to because she got so lost in the beauties of the world. Her favourite plant was the Glow-beam, a beautiful yet deadly flower that killed with the slightest touch. Her mother always said she was like the flower, and years later, Alleria finally knew why. It was her mother's way of telling her the truth, albeit not fully. But it had been a hint all along.

CHAPTER 7

Tanyth and Aiwen fell behind Alleria and her mother, letting their fingertips skim each other from time to time. Aiwen was sure Alleria knew of their secret, but still felt guilty for *betraying* her. How would she feel knowing her two closest friends were together? And how would Pyria react?

"Do you think we should tell her?" Aiwen asked. His eyes didn't leave his tattered boots as he spoke, unable to concentrate on anything else.

"I do," Tanyth said to Aiwen's shock. "But not now. She just found out that her father was murdered, and that she's some sort of prophet. I don't know how she would feel knowing her dearest friends have been lying to her too."

"Agreed." Aiwen squeezed Tanyth's hand in

his, relishing in the proximity, and pulled away just in time for Alleria to turn.

"Everything alright?" She asked.

"Yes, are you?"

"I will feel better once we are out of this place."

"Couldn't agree more."

Alleria turned her head back and settled it on her mother's side. Her dark hair was tied back. However, it still brushed along her mother's frail body.

"ALLERIA SEEMS TO HAVE FORGIVEN PYRIA quickly," Tanyth said, less of a statement, more of a question. His eyes flitted to Aiwen, who was peering back.

"I think she wants to be annoyed with her. But she needs people right now. And if she's going to forgive anyone right now, it is going to be her mother."

Nodding, Tanyth relaxed his body and sighed. "Family is tiring."

"I think this walk is slightly more tiring."

"Oh, I know something *else* that is even more tiring." Tanyth winked.

Aiwen tried not to laugh, but he couldn't hold

in his mighty guffaw. They were supposed to be quiet, not attracting unwanted attention.

Alleria spun around to them again, alarm in her eyes. "What do you two not understand about quiet conversations only?" She was by their side in seconds, pulling them forward to Pyria. "We stick together now. We don't know if anything heard your *fuss*."

"Sorry," Aiwen said. But he was soon interrupted. "What was that?"

CHAPTER 8

Alleria faltered back and at that moment, the towering trees seemed to sway. Then they shook. She flinched at the sudden movement. The muscles in her legs tightened without warning. If needed, she was ready to run.

"WEAPONS!" Pyria shouted. She climbed off Blanchy, a newfound fire trembling in her eyes. With no reluctance, the group unsheathed their weapons and formed themselves in a circle enclosing Blanchy inside.

Something was coming.

"ARE YOU SURE YOU CAN FIGHT?" ALLERIA ASKED. But she already had her answer. Pyria slipped two daggers from each boot and bowed her head. Alleria drew her bow, arrow in place and waited. She held her breath.

Silence. Quiet enough to hear a pin drop.

Until the rustling returned, but louder. As each second passed, it got louder. Louder. Louder. The tree line broke. Four giant wolves flew through the dense terrain, their white fur glistening in the lowlight of the Forest of Malmar.

The group stepped backward, fear trickling through their veins, but their weapons did not falter. The wolves rotated around the circle like they were playing a game. But Alleria would not let them be pawns. She pulled her bow string farther back and surrendered her grip, sending the arrow speeding toward the first wolf. It passed through the bitter air and straight into its stomach. But it did not fall. Instead, the wolf released a grand howl. A deep purple swirled in the wolves' eyes. She remembered the moment she sent out arcs of light that created a purple mist that left the townspeople as they crashed to the floor.

"THEY'RE CORRUPTED!" ALLERIA SAID, DRAWING her bow once again. "Aim for their eyes." With that, Alleria fired another arrow. She watched as

Tanyth jumped forward, axe in hand. The wolf was a metre away when he flung it through the air with all his might, spinning rapidly before crashing into the wolf's side.

Unlike the arrow, the axe was heavy and sent the white creature flying back. But Tanyth wasted no time. He bound forward, ripping the axe from its place and slashing it through the wolf's neck with one swift motion. She saw the blood spewing before something threw her back. So distracted, it had caught her off guard. She screamed as sharp claws pierced her tunic and the soft skin beneath.

FIGHTING OFF UNCONSCIOUSNESS, ALLERIA PUSHED at the wolf's neck with all her force as it snapped its mouth shut over and over. She released one hand from its neck and reached behind her for an arrow. It was stuck under her weight. She yelled an expletive and boosted her body up, grimacing as the claws seeped further into her chest. She pulled an arrow from her quiver before sinking back, the weight of the wolf finally catching up to her.

Gripping the arrow hard, she slammed it through the wolf's eye. She gasped as it pierced through the other side of its skull. She didn't move, scared it was feigning death. It was not until she saw the purple mist leave its eyes, she pushed the dead weight from her, her eyes glassy. The wolf's claws ripped from her body. She released a silent scream and gripped the ravaged hole in her chest. The skin around her eyes bunched as her hand caressed the bloody wound. *Fight through it.* With that, she released her futile grasp, fought to her feet, and scanned her surroundings.

TANYTH RIPPED HIS AXE FROM ANOTHER WOLF'S neck. Her mother was a few strides behind with blood stained daggers unable to do much harm to the violent creatures. Tanyth had to defend her.

Alleria's gaze then latched onto Aiwen, and she was running over in seconds. The final wolf was on top of him, much like her predicament moments ago. Arrows stuck out of every side of the creature, but it was still not down. He screamed as the wolf clamped its mouth shut inches away from his face.

As Alleria ran, she drew her bow and aimed for the head. The arrow was quick but poorly aimed, piercing only the wolf's stomach. "Shit."

Its gaze shot to hers. Howling in pain, it

released Aiwen from its deathly grasp and vanished into the encompassing forest.

It took no time before they were all at Aiwen's side. Tanyth gently raised his head and propped it on his crossed legs. His chest was bleeding, but it didn't seem too deep.

"You all fought well," Pyria said, intercepting the repeated, 'are you okay.' She wiped her daggers on her now ripped trousers and deposited them back in her boots. "Well, it seems Naesaela's magic *can* penetrate the forest's ancient wards."

"Isn't that just typical?" Alleria said. "We need to find some water to wash our wounds. Infection is the last thing we need right now."

"Here," Aiwen said as he threw his water flask at her.

She caught it in her hands, wasting no time unscrewing the lid.

"Thank you," she said. "But my point still stands. We're going to need to find more water."

"Hopefully, we'll find some on the way."

"Hopefully." She thought about suppressing her scream, but anything that wanted to attack them would have heard their fight already. Alleria poured a negligible amount of water on the gash and rubbed it appropriately. She flung the container back to Tanyth, who cleaned Aiwen's wounds.

"The wolf will be back," Pyria said through Aiwen's wails of pain.

"We will be ready this time," Aiwen said once Tanyth finished washing the lesions.

"Therefore, you are my favourite." A slight smirk carved itself on Pyria's usually stern face. They laughed in tow, Alleria included.

"I won't take that to heart," Tanyth said. "You're only saying that because he almost died."

Pyria mounted Blanchy, a modest smirk carved on her face. "Am I?"

Tanyth darted his gaze between Aiwen and Alleria. "I saved her life not even five minutes ago."

"Oh, shut it." Aiwen playfully patted his face. "Take the joke."

"Jokes always have gone straight over your head, Tan," Alleria said as she hoisted Aiwen to his feet, laughing as she did so. He was weak but could still walk, albeit not hastily.

CHAPTER 9

Aiwen's hindered speed was somewhat of a blessing in disguise. For the first time, Alleria could appreciate the forest's beauty. They roamed through dense thicket to meadow-like openings, and never once did any of them complain. Instead, they relished in the nature and calm before the storm.

Tanyth had been trying to get Pyria to recount stories of Aralva, much to her dismay. She had always been secretive over her life before Alleria's birth, but she just accepted it as her mother's business and hers only. Now, Alleria knew why, and she would be a liar if she said it didn't put a sour taste in her mouth. She knew she couldn't stay bitter with her mother forever, but her lies would never go overlooked.

• • •

After endless nagging, Pyria finally gave in to Tanyth's questions. "If I tell you something, will you please be quiet?" She said, jokingly. She dropped her face into her hands and then peered at him.

"Yes, yes, of course. Yes," he said. His mouth geared into a grin, as did Alleria's and Aiwen's.

"Very well," she said. "Many moons ago, like us right now, your father and I were venturing across Malmar. But unlike us, we were not in search of anything in particular. That was, until we stumbled across Aralva: a feat only a handful of humans had done before. Upon our arrival, we were revered—"

"Why revered?" Tanyth interrupted.

Pyria shot him a deathly glare before returning to her story. "Because it is so uncommon for any creature to find Aralva, let alone a human. We were treated like royalty. They gave us a charming home in the village and the opportunity to settle in a place we assumed was a childhood superstition. We only intended to stay for a few weeks, but soon those weeks turned into months and months to years. Two years later, you were born."

• • •

Alleria's mouth gaped. How had she suppressed this her whole life? "Are my grandparents alive?" She snapped, promptly locking her mouth not realising she said it aloud and not in her head. Pyria's face was a picture. Alleria had her answer, but her mother spoke anyway.

"Both your father's parents and mine died when we were young. That is why we travelled like we did; we had nothing to tie us down. But, when we reach Aralva, I hope I can introduce you to the people who were there for us when we needed them. Ayen being one of them."

Alleria forced a smile.

"Pyria, are there any customs or things we need to know before we arrive at Aralva?" Tanyth asked. At that moment, Aiwen perked up, not wanting to miss anything she said. He had always been an eager learner. When he was just eight he had learned which wild berries were edible and which were… not. It had given their families another source of nutrition when things got dire.

Pyria discreetly mouthed her thanks to Tanyth before speaking aloud, "Yes, like most of Malmar, the residents of Aralva look up to the Light. But take care, for they can be radical in their practices.

A single word against the Light, and you will be tried."

All of their eyes widened, not expecting something so grievous to come out of Pyria's mouth. She noted their visible concern and continued with haste. "But you are not to fear. Even if something frivolous was said." She turned to Tanyth, and his cheeks turned crimson in an instant. "You are under Alleria's safeguarding. Nothing will happen to any of you."

"What of you?" Alleria said.

"We can only hope I will be under the same protection." Pyria tried to sound convincing, but Alleria could sense her uncertainty. Maybe her transgressions were too severe for the council to acquit. As strained as their relationship was at that moment, Alleria could not see her mother murdered. It was inhumane. Not to mention, outdated. She would threaten to leave if they did anything to her. It was the only choice.

"Why is Aralva's affiliation to the Light so strong?" Aiwen asked, yearning for further knowledge. Tanyth stifled a laugh, even though it was a valid question. When Aiwen wanted to know something, he wouldn't give in. Luckily, Pyria was no longer keeping secrets.

"Aralva is the epicentre of the Light. Everyone

in Aralva celebrates it and lives by its prophecies." She turned to Alleria. "It is also where your power comes from."

"Why have my powers only just made an appearance? For years, I've been a normal librarian, and then suddenly I'm some sort of prophet." Alleria's voice raised. She was tired of not knowing. Tired of feeling on the outside, even though this was all, seemingly, about her. Why her of all people? She just missed her books. The comfort. The coziness. The sense of normality. Alleria wasn't a fighter. But she'd have to learn to be if she was going to survive.

"Because before, your powers were not needed." Pyria latched onto Alleria's shoulder. "No one knows how the Light works. But like myself, it wanted you to have an ordinary life for as long as you can."

"If my power is channelling the Light, how did I summon that ice storm in the library?"

"That, I am not sure," Pyria said. "However, I can only guess your power was somehow intercepted by Naesaela's magic in an attempt to *kill* you. She is not powerful enough yet, so she took a shortcut. And that shortcut happened to be infecting your power."

. . .

ALLERIA FELL SILENT AND DIDN'T SPEAK FOR THE rest of the day. Soon, darkness cloaked the forest, and they had to set up camp. Alleria attempted to summon some light to help them, but it was no use. The ancient magic of the forest still dampened her power. A saviour who can't even access her power. *Typical,* she thought, practically laughing at their luck.

They found a small stream with water as clean as they could wish for a few hours ago. The pain dwindled, but she surrendered a quick yelp as the water licked the lesion. Aiwen, however, seemed to struggle more. Alleria watched as Tanyth washed his wound for him in the low light of the woodland. She quickly clambered her way to the boys and gripped Aiwen's arm to give him the comfort he needed.an encouragement for him not to scream and declare their location.

"You are so strong," she said into his ear. Keeping quiet was still a priority, and Alleria tried her best to encourage him not to scream and declare their location. She knew if his friends from Elorin saw him like this, he would never live it down. But she never had liked his friends from the market. Aiwen didn't seem to like them that much either, for that matter. It seemed they were only friendly because his stall was next to theirs.

After a few more moments, Tanyth wiped the wound one last time and wrapped it up with a piece of torn cloth. It wasn't until he got up to fetch his bag that Alleria noticed the torn fabric was part of Tanyth's shirt. She craved to make it a spectacle and announce how lovely it was to ruin his only shirt. But she didn't. It didn't seem right to make it a bigger deal than it needed to be. *They will tell me when they're ready,* she reminded herself. Instead, she pulled Aiwen in and settled his head on her lap, where moments later, he slept soundly.

"Great job, you two," Pyria whispered. She dismounted Blanchy and forged a makeshift bed out of some of the broader leaves she must have collected on the way. "He's a strong one, that one." She tipped her head at Aiwen. "That is why he is my favourite."

Tanyth jerked his head around before nonchalantly turning back, pretending like it didn't bother him.

Alleria smiled, finally realising how lucky she was. No, her life wasn't perfect. She was literally on the run. And if she had to have her life turned upside, she was glad it was with her favourite people.

"What is the plan from here?" Alleria asked. Technically, she should be guiding them. After all, it was her fault they were in this situation. However, she knew her mother would ultimately step in and decide their path for herself. But she didn't mind. If anything went wrong, it would fall on her shoulders. And that was a risk she had to take. She was the saviour now. Whether she believed in herself was another question.

"I think we all need to get some rest," Pyria said, already lying down. "We are far away enough that we should not need a lookout. All of you need to get some sleep while we can."

WHILE WE CAN, ECHOED IN ALLERIA'S HEAD AS SHE sought to fall asleep. It should not have sounded as ominous as it did. Pyria and Tanyth were sound asleep and so peaceful. Alleria envied them. For them, sleep was an escape, a liberation from the terrors of reality. Her slumber was a postponement of the nightmare they now faced. More horrors awaited in Aralva, and only the Light knew what else. The dark night sky brightened to an early morning glow when she finally drifted to sleep, her hand still grasping Aiwen.

EVERYTHING WAS BLACK.

Aralva was in ruins, no people or creatures in sight. The clock tower was the only thing that stood, albeit charring and falling apart, its face still without hands. What did it mean? When she tiptoed forward, she felt a crack and crumble beneath her feet. It disturbed the eerie silence. Lifting her foot from the origin of the sound, she found a rib cage. She yelped in horror and lurched backward.

THE GROUND WAS NO LONGER BLACK. BONES covered every inch of Aralva that Alleria could see. Was this truly their future? Death?

Another crack sounded behind her. She jutted her body around to find—

"Aiwen?" She said. "How are you here?"

His eyes drowned in terror, clearly as unsettled and bewildered by the sight as Alleria was.

"Is this…" He trailed off before he could finish his sentence. He was in shock, and for a good reason.

"This is Aralva," She said. "Or *will* be Aralva? I'm still not sure, but how are you here?"

"I don't know. All I remember was falling asleep on your lap, and then this."

Just then, the *dream* seemed to falter. Flashes

of the present Aralva cut through the nightmare fuelled illusion. Bright green peeked through the horizon before fading into darkness once again. A glimpse of Aralva before this *destruction*.

ALLERIA WANTED TO PACE AND THINK, BUT SHE couldn't bear to hear another bone crack. Instead, she studied the black sky. Without looking down, she eventually spoke, "Maybe because I was touching you when I fell asleep, you somehow intercepted the magic that allows me to see these dreams or visions. Whatever they are."

When Alleria lowered her head, Aiwen was next to her. The bones had disappeared.

"That makes sense," he said. His voice was gruffer, like he hadn't spoken for a while.

"What happened?"

"You tell me. It's your dream."

Then she realised his eyes dulled and no longer were the hazel she knew her whole life. Instead, purple swirled.

"Aiwen?"

"Oh, sweet, sweet Alleria. You know I am not Aiwen."

NAESAELA.

Alleria stepped backward.

Back.

Back.

Back.

Only a few lengths separated them now.

"I am not here to harm you, Alleria. Just to give you a message."

Alleria jerked her hands around her body in search of a weapon, of anything. "What is your message?"

Naesaela chuckled, causing Alleria to reach for her bow.

"It is but a simple message." His voice was smooth, yet ragged. Gentle but vicious. *Familiar* but so distant. "There is no use in trying to stop me. You, Alleria Valrona, will perish, and so will your so-called *family."*

CHAPTER 10

Alleria and Aiwen both woke with a stagger. Their gazes clashed, and by the look in his eyes, Alleria knew Aiwen heard what Naesaela said. They would all die. It wasn't a threat. It was a promise.

The early dawn light was breaking through the dense thicket, casting the wooded area in a luminous haze. Glad it was finally daytime, Alleria felt safer, for she didn't like not being able to see what was in front of her. Ironic, given the circumstances. She wasted no time waking up Tanyth and Pyria, then spent the next few moments catching them up.

"So you're telling me Aiwen entered your dream?" Tanyth asked. She was certain she could hear a tinge of jealousy in his tone.

"Yes, for a moment. Naesaela overcame my being. I couldn't speak. Only listen. I was a prisoner in my own body." Aiwen said.

Alleria peered at her mother, hoping she would have something significant to add. Somehow, she still looked ethereal, even after hours of hibernation.

"That is good to know," Pyria said softly. "It shows your powers are manifesting, and you can, somewhat, share them with others. It's valuable."

"Do you think I could distribute my power to others?"

"That, I am not sure. But I do not see why you wouldn't in the future." She brushed her hands through her hair and scaled to her feet. "Once we arrive in Aralva, you will train with the best sorcerers in the land. They know a lot more than I do."

The idea of sorcerers made Alleria's heart skip a beat. She couldn't believe her childhood stories were not stories at all. It made her wonder if any other books from the library were not really fiction. Maybe her past wasn't the only thing hidden from her.

"I think we need to be on our way. We've been dormant for hours now, and the wolf surely would have followed our scent." Tanyth was already on his feet, fully dressed, with his axe sheathed on his back. He had changed from the boy Alleria always knew. Still as sarcastic as ever, but now with a newly found openness. He had never been great at displaying his emotions. But that seemed to have shifted slightly.

"Well, you're keen," Alleria muttered while hoisting her boots on.

"Just to be safe. We saw how much damage those wolves did yesterday."

Alleria pretended not to notice Tanyth's drifting gaze toward Aiwen and the subtle air kiss that followed. Obviously, it wasn't subtle enough. She wished they would tell her.

FIVE MINUTES LATER, THEY MADE THEIR WAY DUE north through the forest. Gathering their bags, they let Aiwen ride Blanchy while he recuperated. By the end of the day, they should reach open land again. Alleria felt hesitant traversing in such an open area. As enigmatic and unfamiliar as the forest was, it did provide some protection.

Pyria drew Alleria back a few lengths. "How are you holding up?" she asked, wrapping her arm around her daughter's shoulder.

"As well as I can," Alleria said. She couldn't

stop twiddling her thumbs. A nervous habit she had since she was younger.

"Understandable,"

"Can we talk about something else? Just for a moment?" Alleria pleaded. "I just need a distraction."

Her mother tightened her lip into a faint smile. "So, Aiwen and Tanyth?" Her head tipped toward the boys in front of them. Tanyth walked beside Blanchy as Aiwen rode atop. Their hands skimmed each other. They must have thought it appeared accidental. Alleria smiled from ear to ear.

"They haven't told me explicitly, but I assume so. They seem to think they're great at hiding it... they're not."

"Indeed. But how do you feel about it?" Her mother replied, chuckling.

"Me? Well, my feelings aren't relevant. Love is a natural *and* an unpredictable situation. And if it manifests between my two best friends... so be it."

Pyria grinned, baring her pearly white teeth. Alleria had not seen her mother smile like that in a long time. Maybe ever.

"They *are* cute together," Pyria said finally. "That is what the youth are saying nowadays, right?"

"So cute," Alleria said instantly. They giggled quietly, and for the first time since leaving for Aralva, they finally looked like a mother and daughter.

"Come on, they will be wondering what we are doing."

With that, they jogged to the boys and formed a line formation so they could all talk openly.

"Well, thank you for joining us," Tanyth said sarcastically. His golden curls still bounced in the sun, even after days of unrest. Maybe *he* was the saviour. He definitely had the hair for it.

"We thought you *must* be missing our presence."

Tanyth snorted a bit too loudly. Pyria shot him a glare, which in turn made Alleria laugh.

"This is why you do not travel with children," Pyria said.

"We are twenty years old," Tanyth said.

"Then act like it—"

A RUSTLING OF LEAVES INTERRUPTED PYRIA.

Silence.

Silence.

Silence—

Before they could react, a wolf tore through the tree-line. Bloodied arrows pierced every side of the wolf. It had followed them and lingered until they least suspected. It lurched forward, its mouth agape, ready to snap toward Alleria.

In a hurry, Tanyth threw his bag into the creature's mouth to buy them some time and pulled his axe from its sheathed position. The beast struggled to release the bag from its mouth, giving the group time to draw their weapons and draw closer. Tanyth lifted the axe, and in one swoop—the white wolf pushed him back. It released the bag and immediately charged. Tanyth fell to the floor with a thump and did not get back up. Both Aiwen and Alleria launched their arrows, but they both missed. The wolf stalked away from Tanyth and toward Pyria, the easiest target, as they drew a second arrow. Snarls filled the once serene forest. With every step back, the wolf pulled closer, not even wincing as arrows struck its body. It wasn't an animal. It was a beast.

"AIM FOR THE EYES!" ALLERIA SAID.

It was no use.

Alleria pulled a blade from her boot and dashed forward. At that moment, the beast growled and pounced toward her mother. She watched as she attempted to duck out of the way, but was slammed to the ground. Wriggling, she tried to angle her daggers toward the beast. But after a sudden jolt, they fell from her hands. The wolf had her limbs pinned to the ground, and all she could do was wait for help.

Alleria stumbled over as she ran to her mother, falling to the sodden grass with a thump. Her ankle roared in pain but she didn't divert her gaze away. Pyria winced as the wolf's snout brushed against her face, and its mouth parted to show it's murderous teeth. It was only when it moved back slightly did she swing her face to Alleria and cry 'Innai.' It was muted by the wolf's guttural snarls, but just loud enough to be made out. It was a desperate cry and a sign of knowing. A sign she knew her fate.

Before Alleria could clamber back to her feet, the wolf lurched onto Pyria's neck. All she could do was watch as her mother's throat was shredded and ripped inside out. Her body went limp, her hands unclenching from the beast's side. And a lone tear fell as the light escaped her eyes.

Alleria couldn't move. So Aiwen did. He drew his arrow once more and let go. It sailed through the air, quickly piercing the wolf's eye. Instantly, it fell to the floor.

Dead.

. . .

A BLANKET OF SILENCE SHROUDED THE ATMOSPHERE until a blood-curdling scream ripped it away. Alleria's. Like time had unfrozen, she shot forward and sank to her knees beside her lifeless mother. She planted her hands on the bloody wound to stem the trickling blood, but it was no use. She died almost instantaneously, and her eyes still emitted the fear from that moment. She didn't die peacefully or on her own terms. She died in horror of being mauled and with question of her daughter's survival. White fur was glued with blood to her mother's hands, signalling how perilous she fought to stay by Alleria's side. Many people would have given in to the temptress of death. But not Pyria. She had fought for her life--for Alleria's freedom. She was not ready to give it up. But she was forced to.

The Aralvan council would presumably be content, for they finally had their 'justice.' Alleria's stomach turned at the thought, and her eyes watered. She cried for her mother, and she cried for herself. She had no biological family left. She was alone. Her stomach turned and her shoulders clenched as her body reeled. She had no biological family left. She was alone.

Innai.

Alleria's mind replayed, working to remember where she had heard the name. Until she realised. The map. Innai was the village closest to the edge of the forest. Pyria must have wanted them to stop there. But she would cross that bridge when they got to it.

Numb to everything and everyone. She couldn't hear Aiwen's desperate cries for her to help. Her body was a prison she couldn't escape from, and she no longer cared. What life was worth living without her mother? Her mind pounded over and over until finally it coiled around her. She heard the yells first. And then recognised Aiwen's tone. All sound suddenly rushing back. She wiped her bloodstained hands on her trousers and scaled to her feet. At that moment, her eyes met with Tanyth's inert frame. She had been so caught up in the madness Tanyth had slipped her mind. She rushed toward him. Aiwen was already checking his pulse. His eyes lifted as Alleria fell to her knees beside him.

"He has a pulse," he finally said. Alleria's heart skipped a beat. Thank the Light. She could not lose two people in one day. "He hit his head, so he will presumably be out for a while."

That was when Alleria saw the blood. Viscous liquid pooled on the ground by his head, and a rock, which was also tarnished red.

"We will set up camp here then and, with any luck, be out of this forest tomorrow morning."

Aiwen nodded his head before dropping it. She needed to say something.

"Aiwen, he will be fine." She seized his hand and gripped it tight. His palms were warm. "I know how much he means to you. I will do anything in my power to make sure he is ok."

He was in tears by the time Alleria finished speaking. He squeezed her hand and let out a sigh.

"I'm sorry about your mother. But you do not need to act strong for me," he spoke tenderly.

She half-smiled, trying not to crane her head toward her lifeless body. Part of her couldn't bear to see her mother like that. But the other needed to.

"I can't talk about it right now," Alleria said. She could not break down. Not when they were this far.

He inclined his head. "I think Blanchy ran off with all the commotion."

Alleria turned her neck to look, carefully passing over her mother. Indeed, Blanchy was gone.

"Good for her. By the Light, if I could run right now… I would." she said, her timbre gravelly. A lot of their bags were on the mare's back. "If we require supplies, there should be a village not too far from the edge of the forest." A lot of their bags were on the mare's back. It wasn't ideal, but she couldn't blame the animal.

THE DAY PASSED SLOWLY. AIWEN STILL COULD NOT lift much, so he skinned the wolf. They might as well get some fresh rations from it. While he prepared food, Alleria dug a grave. If they still had Blanchy, she would have taken Pyria's body with them. But alas, she utilised Tanyth's axe to excavate a shallow hole. When she was done, she and Aiwen split her mother's weight and lowered her down.

"We can say some words when Tanyth is awake," Aiwen said, more of a question than a statement.

Alleria nodded. With everything in her, she fought back cries. She had to stay strong. That was what her mother would want her to do. They were never exceptionally loving toward each other, but her mother cared about her more than anything. She sacrificed herself so that her daughter grow up and have a normal life, in an ordinary town. Now, Alleria wondered how she could have been angry with her in the first place.

Yes, she was taken aback by the lies, but she did it for a reason. For her.

Tanyth finally woke the following day. Aiwen tried not to seem too joyous, but he couldn't help himself. He kissed Tanyth's forehead without a second thought and only withdrew to glance at Alleria. All she did was nod her approval.

"How are you feeling?" Aiwen asked, spinning back around. He studied every part of Tanyth's body for any persistent bleeding and then again.

"Like I hit my head on a rock because an abnormally large wolf threw me backward."

"Good to know it didn't knock the sarcasm out of you," Alleria said.

Tanyth lifted his head, squinting in pain with the release of pressure from the back of his head. He glanced around, and his brow furrowed.

"Where's Pyria?" His eyes locked with Alleria's, and he instantly knew. "No."

Before she knew it, Tanyth was on his feet and had his arms around her, clutching with all his might, which was not too hard thanks to his injury. Alleria was still sore and the added pressure would have been too much. She might have been the saviour, but she wasn't invincible.

"She was the bravest woman I've ever known," he said. "And she will forever live on inside of you and all of us," He pointed at Alleria's chest and then his. "Where do you think you got all this courage from?"

"That is all my mother."

"Of course, it is."

She pulled away and stared at her mother's grave. "Now that you're awake, can we say a few words to send her off?"

Tanyth nodded. They sauntered over. For the next hour, they shared stories and memories of Pyria. Aiwen spoke of a time where she had caught him and Alleria sneaking out to practice their archery. Tanyth recalled when he had given her too little timber at the mill and the wrath he received from her for the following weeks. It never really made sense why she was so angry about that. But that was Pyria. There was nobody like her. She had always been an adversarial person, and she would never forget if you went against her. Even if it was by mistake. But she was also the most loving woman you could meet.

"Do you remember when she would take us to the ocean?" Alleria said.

"Every weekend." Tanyth replied, chuckling.

Alleria didn't face him, but she could picture his face without needing to. Whenever Tanyth laughed, his whole face scrunched together. So much so, his eyes practically became obscured. "I miss it." She finally said.

"She wanted us to see more of Malmar than just Elorin." Aiwen said. "No one else our age ever got to leave Elorin."

"I never realised that." Tanyth said. "Maybe that was her way of letting you into her life more. About her past."

"How so?" Alleria said.

Tanyth scratched his head. "Well, Pyria said she travelled a lot. So maybe, she took us to the ocean, so we could travel too. She obviously enjoyed it."

Alleria nodded. "I guess."

THAT NIGHT, WHEN ALL THREE OF THEM LAY NEAR each other, examining the stars through the thick treeline, Alleria finally gave in to her queries.

"She was thrilled for both of you," she said, turning to the boys. Their faces were pure shock, a sight Alleria revelled in. It was about time.

"She knew?" Tanyth asked, his blinking rapid.

"She asked me earlier today. It seems you weren't subtle enough."

Aiwen looked at Tanyth, genial, and then twisted to Alleria. "Are you ok with this?"

"I'm more than *ok* with it. I want you to be

happy, and I don't care if it's with each other. Just next time, tell me sooner!" The last part came out more aggressively than she expected, but the point still remained. She was immensely happy for them, but hated that they felt the need to hide their relationship from her.

The boys bowed their heads.

"Sorry about that," Tanyth said, gnawing on his bottom lip. "We wished to tell you before we left on this *adventure,* but you were going through so much—"

"It's fine, I promise. I love you both, and nothing or nobody is going to change that,"

"I love you too."

"And so do I," Aiwen said. They lay in silence for a few more moments before Aiwen spoke again. "So, *when* did you know?"

"Aiwen, just because I said I love you doesn't mean I won't thrust this bag at your face." Her hand rested on the bag beside her. She winked. "It is late… and I am tired."

He whispered a virtually imperceptible "sorry" and settled back down, chuckling to himself.

She was, in fact, tired, but she wasn't sure if she could sleep with all her inner quarrels. How could she sleep knowing her mother wouldn't be there when she woke? How could she rest knowing she would, most likely, be subjected to more of Naesaela's nightmares?

After a few minutes, Alleria realised she had neglected to inform them of the *Innai* revelation. She had been so caught up in everything.

"Before she was... killed, my mother said something." She halted her speech for a moment, and listened to the blanket of stifling silence that encapsulated them. "Innai."

No response.

She turned to the boys already asleep, their bodies slumped against each other. Tanyth's face was nestled into Aiwen's neck. They were delightful together, but she would never tell them that. It would get to their heads. Especially Tanyth's. Her stomach warmed at the sight of them, happy they could *finally* be happy themselves. Alleria grinned to herself and turned back over. She stared off into the dark, wooded abyss, still unnerved by what was to come.

CHAPTER 11

Night came and went; Alleria did not sleep. Instead, she waited and watched the rising morning light dance through the tree tops. For hours, she awed in the beauty of nature, and for the first time since they left for Aralva, she forgot about everything. Her mind was devoid of doubt. She pondered when the flowers would germinate and how the garden at her home was doing. It seemed silly, but she hoped it would rain so all the plants wouldn't die. But then it hit her.

How could she return to her family home without a mother? Without a family. Everything would be a perpetual reminder of her brutal death. Her thoughts turned sour, and the past few hours finally caught up with her.

In frustration, she ripped the grass from where her hands lay. The boys must have sensed her anguish, for they awoke not long after. Alleria's eyes were bloodshot and tired.

"Rough night?" Tanyth asked, rubbing his eyes as he did so. At least somebody got a good night's sleep. One of them would need to be alert today.

"I couldn't sleep," Alleria said. She reached for the leftover food and ate. "I just couldn't bear any more nightmares." She stuck out her hand, offering them some food. They both shook their heads.

"I don't think being stuck inside this forest is helping." Aiwen's voice was gravelly from his slumber.

"I assume a few more hours, and we're out."

"Thank the Light."

TWENTY MINUTES LATER, THEY WERE HEADING north again. Alleria kept hope that Blanchy would return. The mare was the only thing in a close radius that reminded Alleria of her mother, and she didn't want to lose that, even if it was *just a horse.* Pyria had bought Blanchy when Alleria turned five. Still, to this day, she didn't know how her mother afforded a horse, and now she never would.

Tanyth and Aiwen walked closer now, which made Alleria genuinely smile. They still didn't let their hands touch for more than a second or two, but she was glad they felt comfortable enough to do that much. She never had a relationship like that. She wasn't sure if she ever would. Growing up, she knew she was interested in boys and girls and everything in-between. But at twenty years old, she realised she didn't want a relationship like most people did. She wanted to love someone for *them* and their personality and soul. Not for their body and what lies underneath. She wasn't interested in that. Maybe she would be one day after meeting the right person. But for now, she was happy as she was.

"SO, WHAT IS THE PLAN AFTER WE'RE OUT OF THE forest?" Aiwen asked.

"We're heading straight to Innai," Alleria said, not taking her eyes off the path in front, scared her tired feet would drive her to trip.

"Innai?" Tanyth said. "I don't think I've heard of it."

So they definitely were asleep when she'd mentioned it last night. As much pain as it brought her to relive those harrowing moments, she told them of what her mother said.

"Why do you think she wants us to go there?"

"I don't know, but I don't think it's very big. Probably just a riverside village that deals a lot in treasure from river excursions and general goods."

Tanyth laughed. "How much *treasure* could be in the river?"

"Malmar is millions of years old," Alleria replied. Her tone was unexpectedly brash. She continued softly. "There is treasure all around us. You just need to know where to look. But *that* is for another day." Tanyth couldn't suppress his interest, to which Aiwen laughed.

EVERY TIME A TREE SHOOK IN THE WIND, OR A mouse scurried across the forest floor, Alleria jumped. She considered drawing an arrow, just to be safe, but decided against it. She couldn't live in fear. Otherwise, her mind would spiral. She already knew her emotion controlled her power, but she didn't want to see what it would be like if her thoughts weren't coherent.

Another rustle sounded, but it sounded different this time, close enough for Alleria to pull her bow from her back and draw an arrow.

Aiwen did the same, and Tanyth unsheathed his axe. The trio were a band of soldiers, stricken with grief, but ready for whatever came their way.

Suddenly, another wolf appeared through the overgrown woodland. But it was bigger. A lot bigger. Its eyes blazed the same deep purple as the others, but a gnarlier mouth surrounded them. Its teeth peeked through as it snarled and drew closer to them. It seemed to grow. Alleria's eyes widened when she finally realised. They had been so bewildered by its horrifying face they hadn't seen its sly steps toward them. Closer and closer.

Now mere lengths away, Alleria finally shot her arrow. It sliced through the wintry morning air and straight through the ear of the beast. With that, it howled and lunged forward. Alleria saw Aiwen's arrow fly but miss the wolf entirely.

"BY THE LIGHT... ANOTHER WOLF?" TANYTH shouted, throwing his axe in tow. It spun for a moment before burying itself in the beast's side. Not to their surprise, it didn't go down. Instead, it howled. The wound didn't remotely hinder the beast. Tanyth grunted, strode toward Alleria, and drew her blade from her boot. "Plan B." She tried to stop him, but there was little she could do. He'd had enough.

The wolf dodged every arrow that flew toward it. Alleria and Aiwen stepped back, allowing themselves more distance to aim. But Tanyth had somehow snuck behind the beast, and in a swift motion, he jumped. He was on the wolf's back as it writhed to get him off. With one arm, he held on, and with the other, he slammed the dagger over and over into its head.

"How is it still conscious?" Aiwen said, his words quickening whilst still trying not to bring any attention back to them. He watched in horror as his lover clung to the wolf's body. "What do we do?"

Alleria's brows furrowed as she thought.

Think.

Think.

Think.

"The arrows seem to only work in the eyes," She said finally. "We need to get closer."

They took no time in strategising, which they perhaps should have, and sprinted toward the beast, their bows drawn. They fired. The possessed creature jumped. Tanyth flew back and onto the hard ground below, his eyes shut. Before they could react, the wolf struck Aiwen. He flew without grace, but she didn't see him hit the ground. Alleria ran, knowing she was dead if she didn't move now. She slipped away into the tree-line.

SHE RAN WITH AS MUCH MOMENTUM AS SHE COULD, not even pausing when she crashed into the trees. She would return for her friends once the wolf was off her trail. She had to do something. Fast. Without shifting her neck, she knew by the rustling in the trees that it was behind her. The grisly snarls and substantial steps sent quivers down her spine. If she stopped just for one second, she would have been dead. All this would have been for nothing. She would have lost her mother. For nothing--

Light crept through gaps in-between the trees. It grew brighter and brighter until she was out.

She was out of the forest.

But on a cliff.

She had run east instead of north. *Shit*. She approached the edge and looked down. The River Tarron awaited her, and at that very moment, it was her best and only option. She had a better chance with the deadly currents than—

A snap of a twig invaded her hearing, and her head shot around. The wolf was closing in, lazily stalking toward her. The ground shook with every step it took. It was playing with her. But it was a game Alleria willed to play. It was now or never.

She emptied her mind of all concern and worry and let the scent of the forest overcome her. *Be brave.* "Fuck *you,*" she said calmly, a smirk spreading on her face.

At that moment, she lunged off the cliff, spinning in her wake. She drew an arrow and, with alacrity, let it go. Her last sight of the wolf was the the terror on its face as Naesaela's magic escaped it. As she fell, maybe to her death, Alleria looked skyward toward her mother and awaited impact.

CHAPTER 12

The sun began to set by the time Tanyth woke up. He wobbled to his feet, unbeknownst to what had transpired. Squinting, he gazed over the area, praying his friends would be fine. He spotted Aiwen quickly after, passed out. Soon, he was on his knees, hoisting his lover's head up and coaxing him awake, the smell of ichor permeating the air.

"Aiwen, wake up," he said, a sense of brewing dread percolating into his tone. With every word, his urgency heightened until he was near enough shouting.

"AIWEN, IT IS TIME TO WAKE UP." He shook him as tears streamed down his battered face.

He and Aiwen had always been friends, but it

wasn't until a year ago when it surprisingly evolved to something else. Tanyth asked Aiwen to accompany him in collecting timber for the mill because of increased sightings of bears in the area. Aiwen *was* a lot better with a bow than himself.

They had been collecting timber for an hour when three black bears appeared. Instead of attacking, the boys slumped behind some trees to wait them out. They don't know how it happened, but before they knew it, Tanyth's lips were brushing Aiwen's neck, and then his face, and then…

AIWEN'S EYES SHOT OPEN, AND HE RELEASED A mighty cough. Bruises littered his face, but the only thing Tanyth saw were his hazel eyes. Lunging forward, he wrapped his arms around Aiwen, not realising he might be in pain.

"Don't you ever do that to me again," he said into his ear. Tanyth released him from his grasp and pushed his blonde curls from his eyes. He quickly tipped his head back, his eyes closed, and thanked the Light. This could have ended very differently.

"Actually, you got knocked out before me. So don't you ever do that to *me* again." Aiwen brushed his hand against Tanyth's cheek and mouthed 'sorry.' "Where's Alleria?"

Tanyth couldn't hide his surprise, his selfishness. He got so caught up with Aiwen he didn't even think to check for Alleria. Pushing his feet to the ground, he hauled through the twilight. It was still bright enough to see their surroundings, but Alleria was gone. A memory. How long had it been?

"Where is she?" Aiwen asked, finally getting to his feet, his hand against the laceration on his chest, evidently in discomfort.

"Not here."

The boys scurried around the opening and surrounding wooded area, but to no avail. She was gone.

"The wolf wasn't dead when I got knocked out."

"So, she was alone?"

"Yes."

"Shit," Tanyth said, his shoulders curling forward. His chest caved as he thought of her. She shouldn't be alone. Not now. "She would've run into the forest again. It would've been harder for it to follow, but not impossible."

"We'll have to hope she had the sense to carry on north so we can meet her in Innai."

"You actually want to leave?"

"We don't have a choice, Tan. She's out there by herself, and if she's still in the forest… she doesn't have her powers."

Silence followed for a moment until Tanyth gave in. "I hate when you're right," he murmured, tucking his shirt into his trousers. He didn't hide his trembling hands. "I say we leave now then. I can't wait an entire night."

"You read my mind."

❄

ALLERIA PASSED OUT BEFORE SHE HIT THE WATER. She awakened with water crashing against her face and the stench of fish invading her senses. Then, she felt a net between her fingers. It pulled her. Her eyes opened, and as she wiped them, she saw it. A village. She was being dragged to the shore by a fisherman. That was why the smell was so… pungent.

Coughing hard, the water she swallowed slipped from her mouth. Better to do it now than in front of strangers. After a few moments, a hand reached out, pulling her from the perilous depths. Water splashed in her vision as she clambered to the riverside. She felt a towel wrap around her, a burly man standing in front of her. She always was an excellent judge of character, and she already trusted him. His eyes felt kind. Her mother would always tell her to trust her instincts, so she did.

"Thank you," Alleria said through her chattering teeth.

"What were you doing in the river, young one?" Alleria noticed his accent right away. His consonants were strong, and the twang in the words could only mean one thing.

"Did I make it to Innai?"

"You did." He half-smiled, confusion still in his eyes. "But my question still remains."

"It is a long story that I'm willing to tell if we can go inside."

"Of course," he said. "Follow me."

Alleria was hot on his heels, aching to get out of the cold, and hoping he would have a change of clothes. She found herself swallowing her dread over and over. Tanyth. Aiwen. They were still out there.

"What is your name?" he said, not turning around. The man towered over her. But, somehow, she wasn't intimidated. Instead, she felt a weird comfort. Like she *knew* him.

"Alleria." As soon as the words left her lips, she regretted them. How *could* she trust this stranger? What would her mother have though?

He craned his neck. "I'm Alnor."

. . .

As they walked through Innai, people stared, not in distaste but in intrigue. It seemed Innai had few visitors. She dropped her head in embarrassment. She never liked attention.

A few lengths later, Alnor stopped at a large red door and quickly unlocked it, ushering her inside. A woman with twisted black hair was seated, a warm drink in hand. Alnor stepped in front of Alleria.

"Rosa, this is Alleria," he said. "Can you brew us some tea? It seems we're in for a good story."

Alleria came to realise that Rosa was Alnor's sister. She should have guessed by their identical deep brown eyes and matching skin. After letting the tea steep, Rosa gave Alleria some clothes to change into and started the fire.

Alleria told them everything but her destination and 'prophecy.' She could sense their curiosity, noticing the siblings' momentary glances at each other as she recalled what happened. After she finished, they sat in silence. Until Alnor finally spoke.

"I'm sorry about your mother," he said, unusually sombre. Why was he so taken aback? "So, your friends are still in the forest?"

"They are," Alleria replied, praying they were alive.

"You can wait here for them if you please," Rosa added.

Alleria smiled. "That means a lot, but I must go back for them."

A small laugh escaped Alnor. "That is a death wish, Alleria, and besides, it would take nearly a day just to reach the forest."

"I thought it was close to Innai?"

"Maps are nearly always inaccurate, I'm afraid."

Alleria looked from Alnor to Rosa and realised she had no better option. She had no choice. "I think I will take you up on the offer for tonight then."

Rosa reached over, rubbed Alleria's arm and strolled off. Alleria assumed she was preparing a bed. For the first night in days, Alleria might have a better night's sleep. She almost forgot her powers had returned. Maybe her nightmares wouldn't be so intense now.

"I know you're looking for Aralva," Alnor admitted, his voice stern.

Alleria's head turned so quickly, she felt it crack. "How did you—"

"The only thing directly north in Malmar is Aralva."

"You know about Aralva?"

"I do."

Alleria tried to not sound annoyed by his curt response. Her mother must have known somehow. "How?"

Alnor sighed and clamped his hands together. "I was born in Aralva. As was Rosa," he said. "But we left twenty years ago." He focused his eyes on Alleria. Her brows furrowed at the revelation. "When they killed your father."

Alleria felt her chest tighten and her breathing falter for a second. She must have known Alnor was here, that he might be able to help. This was why her mother wished for her to reach Innai.

"Before my mother died, she told me to come here. Did you know her well?"

"My sister knew her through me. But I knew her very well," he said. "We were together."

Alleria jumped from her seat. "I'm sorry?!" She raised her voice so much, Rosa peeked her head in from the other room. Alnor nodded his head at her, and she disappeared.

"Not like that," he said, almost laughing. He unclenched his hands and let them fall into his lap. "There's an ancient rite in Aralva, much like marriage but for friendship. It's a promise to not betray the other and to never turn your back. Hence why I'm living in this insignificant village and not my hometown. I left in respect to your parents. It just felt wrong to live there after what they did to you all."

Alleria fell back to her seat in shock, now lacking the strength to support herself. She felt the hairs on her arms raise. All her life, she thought her mother was incapable of being close to people or having friends. Alnor was definitely not a testament to that.

"How did she know you were here?" Alleria looked at him. "You left *after* my mother, right?"

"That's true," he said. "She knew I was here because she told me to come here if the worst happened. Innai was where your mother was born, Alleria. And your father. This was their home before they left to travel Malmar."

Alleria's eyes wandered around the house. Her father had walked in these very walls. It was probably the closest she had ever been to him. She wouldn't say it aloud, but she suddenly felt like he was with her, reassuring her. Alleria shook her head at the thought. Now was not the time to think about that. People were going to die.

Rosa walked through the door. "I've set up the guest room for you, Alleria. There's a change of clothes and some towels."

"Thank you, Rosa."

"Just get some rest. You've had a precarious

week, by the sounds of it. That goes for you too, Alnor!" She pointed her finger at him and withdrew into what Alleria assumed must be her bedroom.

"She's right," Alnor finally said, standing up. He stretched his arms up and surrendered a yawn. "We need to get some sleep." He strode to the door adjacent to Rosa's, opened it, and, before closing it behind him, said, "Goodnight, Alleria."

The boys were Alleria's only concern. Memories of them plagued her mind for hours after she retired for the night. How was she to know if they had even survived their encounter with that *beast*? As she cradled herself to sleep, she tried to not let her mind wander. Thinking of what was to come would only make things worse. So instead, she forced her eyes shut and let her head sink into the pillow.

CHAPTER 13

"How much further do you think it goes for?"

Tanyth struggled to keep up with Aiwen, his head still pounding from their encounter with the white beast. Aiwen's steps were light and impish to deter from any unwanted attention. Tanyth's not so much. He stumbled every few steps, walking directly through patches of parched, noisy leaves. Aiwen identified some head trauma and asked they settle. But Tanyth insisted on pursuing through the night. Alleria's life depended on it.

"It's hard to say," Aiwen said. He craned his neck to check on his 'boyfriend.' It felt weird for him to say so openly, so he didn't. They had been together for a long while now but hadn't put labels on the relationship. They both hated labels. "From my experience, the drier the leaves, the less light they get. Right?"

"I suppose so?" Tanyth shrugged.

"Meaning they're deeper into the forest where the sun doesn't reach them as well."

"Where are you going with this?"

Aiwen stopped, attentive not to step on any sticks that could give away their whereabouts. He knelt on the floor and picked up a leaf. It was emerald green, and when he twisted it in his hands, it did not crush.

"These leaves are healthy."

"So we're close?"

Aiwen started pacing forward again. The tree-line was so dense, he had to force branches apart to get through. "It seems so."

Suddenly, Aiwen stood still. Tanyth stopped himself before he crashed into him.

"Careful, Ai."

AIWEN MOVED TO THE SIDE, REVEALING WHAT MADE him stop in his tracks. Fields of green blanketed in the delicate shroud of night stunned his senses. They had made it out. The forest and its horrors were finally behind them. Tanyth's face immediately lit up. He ran past Aiwen and out into the fresh air. Aiwen followed, a distressed look on his face.

"Don't overdo it, Tan. Your head—"

"I feel fine," Tanyth interrupted. He touched the back of his head, but didn't wince like he had before. He furrowed his brows in confusion. "It doesn't hurt anymore." He patted it again.

"How weird." Aiwen turned his whole body and peered back into the forest. The parting they escaped through had closed up. No one would know they ever stepped foot. "The forest seems to have a mind of its own." Aiwen turned back to find nothing. Tanyth was gone. He ran forward to where he saw him last. Everything slowed but his heart thumped out of his chest. The fear was unravelling him from the inside out.

Snap.

Aiwen's head shot around. Tanyth stood at the end of a seemingly steep dune, his back facing him. Aiwen's heart didn't slow, not now. Not when he thought he'd lost Tanyth. That wasn't something he could get over so quickly.

"Tan, what the fuck are you doing?" Aiwen

stormed over to him, fury unleashing in every stride.

Suddenly, Tanyth turned.

"What's wrong?" he said, clueless to Aiwen's terror. He scratched at his head.

Aiwen finally reached Tanyth and slightly pushed him before hurling his arms around his torso. "Don't ever do that again." Aiwen sniffled.

Tanyth could sense his worry, so he softened his tone. "Do what?" He spoke with compassion. He didn't lace it with his usual sarcasm or witty remarks. Instead, he placed his index finger beneath Aiwen's chin and raised it from his chest. Their eyes met, and it felt like the first time all over again.

"I turned around, and you weren't there. I can't bear the thought of losing you, not now. Not after what we've gone through these past few days," Aiwen said, stammering every few words. His gaze didn't leave Tanyth's, he kept falling in deeper. He could swim in his cerulean eyes for hours and would if it weren't for the circumstances. He spoke again. His words melded together with the speed he spoke them. "I just panicked.I don't know why because you were right there but I didn't see you. I'm sorry for shouting I just—"

. . .

Tanyth's lips collided with Aiwen's, cutting his 'sentence' short. Aiwen's eyes still widened in disbelief every time their mouths intertwined, and Tanyth's tongue explored his own. He always knew he had no interest in women. Only Tanyth had ever caught his eye. But Tanyth had never shown the same signs, and he'd only been with women growing up. Until that day behind the trees.

Aiwen stopped his mind from spiralling and reminiscing over the past, so he could enjoy the moment. His lust for Tanyth's touch only grew more rampant when he felt his lover's hands grip him from behind. In a frenzy, Aiwen returned the favour. He let his fingers dance across Tanyth's body, now a subject to the sweet temptress of desire.

After a few moments of ecstasy, Tanyth pulled away, smiling.

"As much as I'm enjoying this, we have things to do."

"You still want to walk through the night?

We don't know where we're going." Aiwen would be lying if he said it did not disappoint him that Tanyth wanted to keep walking. He felt so selfish thinking that, but he just couldn't resist when it came to Tanyth. Despite the obscurity of night, his blue eyes still glittered. At that moment, the moonlight struck off them. Before Tanyth could react, Aiwen dived forward. Just a moment more.

Their lips collided once again, and this time, Tanyth didn't stop. Soon, they were lying on the ground, their eyes latched onto each other. Tanyth retrieved a woven blanket from his bag and, wasting no time, wrapped them both in it. He nuzzled closer to Aiwen to preserve heat, pressing his lips against his neck. Aiwen tried to hide the rush he felt, but he couldn't help the shivers that passed through his body. Tanyth trailed slightly upward before resting at his ear. Finally, he whispered. "You're right. We'll seek Innai in the morning."

❄

ALLERIA WAS UP AT THE BREAK OF DAWN. ALNOR had woken her up for the training. Whatever that entailed. He hadn't specified what they'd be training, just that he expected her by the river in thirty minutes. She clambered from her bed promptly, her eyes rested for the first time in almost a week. Finally, she had a good night's rest. She felt alive but couldn't help but think about the boys. Her guilt ate her alive, as she was sure they had an awful night's sleep, if they were even alive. She pinched herself at the thought. *Of course, they're alive,* she thought.

She sauntered to the chest of drawers at the tip of the room. A fresh pair of clothes were laid neatly folded atop. Rosa must have put them here before she had woken up. She should have been freaked out someone entered the room without her knowledge, but they were her mother's friends. She could trust them.

TWENTY MINUTES LATER, SHE LEFT THE HOUSE, finally escaping the grasp of Rosa and her persistence on feeding her. *You'll need the nourishment,* she said. Finally, she had given in and consumed a handful of berries just to please her. But she couldn't help but feel guilty. She hoped the boys had food. Walking through the streets of Innai, she avoided any contact with people in the village. She didn't have the time or the energy to make any more acquaintances.

However, she caught people staring as she passed through. She noted the whispers and didn't bother to try to listen to what they were saying.

Nevertheless, she hoped it wasn't harmful. Ever since she was little, she always needed everyone to like her. Tanyth told her it was a god complex, but Alleria didn't think she was better than everyone else. She just wanted to be accepted by everyone else. They were two different things entirely.

After what seemed like hours, Alleria finally reached the river. Alnor stood, not far from where he saved her the night before, his arms crossed.

"You're late by thirty seconds," he said. Alleria couldn't decipher whether he was joking. She hadn't known him long enough to know if sarcasm was something he was capable of.

"I'm sorry," she replied, just to be safe. To her relief, he laughed.

"You should have seen your face!" His smile was wide, exposing his bright teeth. She hadn't seen him smile before, but she could see why her mother was friends with him.

"Hilarious," she said. She didn't realise she was smiling too. Despite not having her mother or father around, she'd never felt closer to both of them. She finally knew about their past, and she couldn't hide her happiness with that fact. "What are we going to train?"

It was then Alleria noticed the gilded recurve bow that lay near Alnor. He caught her glare and picked it up.

"I assume your power has manifested by now?"

Alleria nodded.

"Great," he said, tracing his finger down the bow and rejoicing in the wood's smoothness. It appeared to be stained with genuine gold. "But you must learn not to rely on your powers. That is where Naesaela will get the upper hand. She will expect you to solely use your magic." He tossed the bow to Alleria. "That is what this is for."

She opened her hand to catch it but watched as it disintegrated before her eyes. A golden light had shot from her palms, and the exquisitely crafted bow was no more. Silence encompassed them both until Alnor's laughter broke through. A great guffaw laced with nothing but joy. No anger at all.

"That was amazing," he said through his howls. Alleria nervously laughed. "I'll admit, you just destroyed a priceless bow and heirloom. But I don't even care. That was incredible—"

"I'm so sorry," Alleria interrupted. Her hand was against her mouth in disbelief at what had just occurred, her stomach tightening. But he didn't care?

"Sorry?! Alleria, you just destroyed something with your bare hands," he said, still laughing.

"You didn't even have to try. By the Light, you were not even touching it! You're so much more advanced than I thought."

"You think I'm strong enough?—"

"I didn't say that," he said, his voice suddenly indifferent. "You're strong, yes. But you still have a long way to go… I just fear we won't have enough time."

Alleria worried this would be the case. She panicked many times over that she would reach Aralva but not be able to help. She would have wasted the journey and lost her mother for nothing. That couldn't happen.

"PLEASE DON'T SAY THAT," ALLERIA SAID, NOT realising she had said it out loud until she saw Alnor's face change.

He closed the gap between them and settled a hand on her shoulder. "I promise you, your mother's death will not be in vain."

Alleria forced a smile and surrendered a mighty sigh. "Ok, what's first?"

"I thought you'd never ask." Alnor smiled. He reached behind a tree stump and pulled another bow from the shadows. Alleria chuckled as he handed it to her. This time, as she reached for it, she slowed her breathing and focused, smiling when she felt the curve of the bow touch her fingers.

"Well, thank the Light for that," Alnor said. "I don't have another, so I'm glad you didn't destroy this one. Your power is very unreliable... erratic, if you will. That's something we'll try to work on."

Alleria let her hands explore the bow. It wasn't as luxurious as the golden one before, but it was beautiful. Worn at the edges but with tremendous character. You could tell a lot about a person by the condition of their bow. She could tell Alnor had owned the bow for a long time and could feel where he had sanded it down to smooth out any imperfections.

"It's a beautiful bow, Alnor."

"Thank you. It's the only bow I've ever used."

"You have... *had* a golden bow, and you didn't care to use it?"

"I'm not one for fancy things. I only had it because I couldn't bear to sell it. It had been in the family for centuries."

Alleria's stomach turned at the thought. She had destroyed a priceless family heirloom, and Alnor didn't seem to mind. "I'm sorry again."

"Things happen," he said. His smile was sincere, so he really must not mind. That alleviated Alleria's guilt a little. "Now, let's get to work."

FOR HOURS, ALNOR AND ALLERIA PRACTISED. After the initial few shots, it had grown stale and mundane, but Alnor insisted she kept firing. She was glad she had because, after a while, she recognised her improvement. Her aim was as precise as it could be. By the end of the training session, Alnor would name something for her to shoot, and she would hit it in its centre in seconds. She had always been good with a bow, thanks to her time hunting. But this was different. Now, she was a marksman.

"I think that's enough of that," Alnor finally said. "Before we finish, I want to try something that'll combine both of your strengths."

"And what's that?"

"Aim your bow toward the river," he said, his gaze drifting to the water. "Not at anything in particular, just at the water."

Alleria did as he said. She pulled an arrow from her quiver and aimed the bow toward the empty, watery landscape. It was serene and the river calm, not like the night before.

"Great," he said. Alleria could sense his excitement. "Now, when you release the arrow, I want you to channel your power and attempt to syphon it *into* the arrow."

"Why?" She relaxed the bow, lowering it as she did so.

"Just think how fast and strong just one arrow could be with your powers."

Alleria didn't mutter another word. Instead, she aimed the arrow again. Inhaling a deep breath, she let her troubles seep from her mind. At that moment, she was merely a girl with a bow, nothing else. She pulled the arrow back and felt the wind crash against her hand, let it go.

Instantly, she raised her hand and forced the warm power that lay dormant inside her stomach up and through her palm. Radiant yellow light escaped its prison in an arc. She squinted her eyes and watched as it syphoned into the arrow. Before her eyes, it flared a vivid gold and shot forward quicker than she'd seen anything move before. It soon soared out of sight; Alleria faltered back, in shock at what she had just accomplished. She didn't see or hear Alnor jumping up and down in glee. She just marvelled at what she was capable of and suddenly was hopeful for the future.

CHAPTER 14

Tanyth woke before Aiwen, to the whisper of a bitter chill tickling his exposed leg. When he finally allowed his eyes to flutter open, he was met with a beautiful early morning light. Flocks of birds circled above, unknowing of the boys' burdens. In that moment, Tanyth envied them, and their innocence. His gaze soon trickled downward to find the blanket completely pulled to Aiwen's side. That explained why he was so cold. Tanyth shot a harsh glare toward Aiwen, which went unseen, and dragged the fleecy material back over himself. He tried to fall back to sleep but couldn't. By the Light he needed it. He yearned for slumber, but the blinding light distracted him too much. He would have to go without.

Instead, he cherished the time he could stare at his lover without judgement from Aiwen himself. Aiwen had never been overtly romantic. But Tanyth had just whittled it down to him being uncomfortable. He always told him he was too sappy, but to Tanyth, that was love. This was Aiwen's first relationship, so Tanyth had made sure they had taken things slowly, even if Aiwen had contested against it. Tanyth had so much respect for Aiwen; he didn't want to take advantage of the situation, or him.

WHEN THE SUN WAS NOT FAR OFF ITS MIDPOINT, Aiwen finally woke from his temporary coma. Tanyth watched as his fingers scraped at his eyes, trying to see if the sun's position was deceiving him. His hair was only slightly unkempt. They both were blessed with unusually tame hair.

"Why didn't you wake me up?" His voice raised, but still unsteady from sleep. Despite his strident tone, Tanyth could secretly tell he was thankful for the extended rest. Smiling, Tanyth reached for his limp hand and yanked him to his feet. He couldn't help but let his eyes wander over his bare chest that was dusted in dark hairs.

"Eyes are up here, Tan—" His words were cut short by his own laughter.

Tanyth's head shot skyward to find Aiwen smirking at him. "You looked like you could do with some more rest," he admitted.

"What's that supposed to mean?"

"Nothing." Tanyth could tell he was joking, but he would play along. "It was just an extremely tiring day and *night.*"

Aiwen giggled at Tanyth's suggestive remarks. He brought the fun side out of him, even if he didn't always recognise and appreciate it in the moment. He liked that. Aiwen knew he could be too serious at times, so Tanyth was the perfect counterbalance. It was well noted that opposites attract, and there were no two more opposing people than them.

Tanyth latched his hand around Aiwen's neck, pulled his face to his own until their chests touched and their faces were inches away from each other. They lingered, their mouths quivering at the intimacy. The tension was practically visible in the morning air; Aiwen bit his lip in anticipation.

"I could kiss you right now," Tanyth said so quietly, only Aiwen would be able to hear. His voice echoed a sweet noise that was so seductive.

"What's stopping you?"

Tanyth pulled his lover's face even closer, their lips as close as they could be without brushing against each other. He let his fingers explore Aiwen's neck, his cheek, and then his bare back. Aiwen's eyes closed so he could savour Tanyth's touch. Whenever they were together, it felt like the first time all over again. He cringed at the thought, but it was the truth. Everyday felt like they grew closer together, but it also scared him. He didn't want to depend on Tanyth, or anyone, for that matter. They had this spark that never whittled, a flaming candle that never burnt out. And just then, their lips collided, the salty taste sending shudders from his spine to his feet. Then it was gone. A rose that germinated, bloomed and withered in a matter of moments. A performance with no ending. He forced his eyes open to find Tanyth a stride backward, his eyes still burning a metaphorical hole into Aiwen's body.

"Now is not the time," Tanyth said, evidently struggling to keep his urges at bay. Aiwen watched as he twitched and forced himself to keep his distance. He resembled that of a fox spying a rabbit. Finally, Tanyth brought himself to continue his words. "We need to set off immediately. If we hurry, we can reach Innai by nightfall. I believe it is downhill from here, so it should be possible."

Aiwen could almost see the desire festering behind his cerulean eyes. He could have easily given in to the temptations that tormented them both. But he was right. They had been selfish and hadn't thought it through properly. They needed to find Alleria right away.

"Do you have everything?" Tanyth was already racing down the steep, dewy hill, his bag in hand. After throwing on his clothes from the day before, Aiwen snatched his bag from the floor, tied it shut, and ran after Tanyth. They strolled side by side, their hands clutched together, intertwined for the remainder of the journey. If time was kind, they could reach Innai within the day. If fate was kind, Alleria would be there.

CHAPTER 15

Alleria dropped the knife.

She wandered back, admiring her handy work. Three carrots, an onion, and some green vegetable she had never seen before were sliced to precision before her. Rosa had got her to help with the food, a stew of some sort. She utilised her newly found dicing skills and got to work with some meat.

The sun was setting, and she'd had no contact with the boys. She tried not to worry, but tomorrow she would have to leave Innai for Aralva with or without them. It was unpleasant to think like that, but Malmar was on the brink of destruction. She hoped they would understand.

"You alright there?" Rosa broke her train of thought. "You're bleeding."

Alleria dropped the knife when she noticed red dripping from her finger. She had gotten so caught up in her own thoughts she hadn't felt the steel grazing her finger. Rosa appeared in her peripheral with a damp cloth in hand. She held it against the wound for a few moments as Alleria tried not to wince. The pain stung like a wasp and caused a dull ache but annoying, nonetheless. It wasn't excruciating, but she was tired of suffering. Ever since the day in the library, her body ached and pleaded for her to slow down, to have some time to herself. But she couldn't. Hurting was a new constant in her life.

The stinging burned, becoming more intolerable with every second that passed.

"Why does that hurt so much?" She asked, her teeth bared.

"Alcohol," Rosa said. She peeled back the cloth to look at the wound and then covered it up again. "Just in case of infection... We don't want our *saviour* falling ill now. Do we?"

Alleria nodded, a smile crawling on her face. "I guess not," she said.

Finally, Rosa removed the cloth to reveal rather a deep gash that had, thankfully, stopped bleeding. "Thank you."

Even though Naesaela seemed to have stopped its torment on Alleria for now, she still seemed to distract her in other ways. She didn't know how much longer she could take it. The nightmares almost seemed better than the waiting and the unknowing.

"TELL ME ABOUT NAESAELA." THE WORDS ESCAPED Alleria's mouth before she could think them over. Now, she just hoped Rosa was as willing to talk about her past as Alnor was. She noticed Rosa's surprise at the mention of the evil's name, but no fear glinted in her eyes. She must share a similar sentiment with her mother when it came to Naesaela. She too was not afraid to speak Naesaela's name, as she had already experienced a fate worse than death. A life that no person should ever have to live.

Rosa inclined her head toward two armchairs tucked in the corner of the room; they both took a seat. Alleria caught Rosa freeing an uneasy sigh from her lips. She almost felt bad for asking her about Naesaela. It seemed to be a taboo subject for the citizens of Aralva. But if Alleria was going to defeat her, she would have to learn everything she could about her.

"I will speak with you about Naesaela until

those potatoes are boiled." Alleria followed her pointed finger to the great pot that sat on an open flame. "Deal?"

"Yes, of course. Deal," Alleria said, stumbling over her words.

"Very well. What do you want to know?"

Alleria started sentences and stopped halfway through multiple times, unsure of what to ask first. So many things flooded her mind; she just couldn't tell what was the most important.

"Where did Naesaela come from?" She blurted out.

"The question of all questions… A question I cannot answer. No one of our time knows. We have our theories but—"

"What's your theory?" Alleria said, interrupting her speech. She didn't say sorry, for she was too eager. Light, she felt like Aiwen in that very moment, always demanding to learn something new.

"Well, my beliefs equate with the ancient scrolls I've read in the Aralvan library. They say Naesaela was once a girl like you and I. However, unlike you and I, she was a sorcerer with a mighty hunger for knowledge. She thirsted for more and more until, one day, the Light decided she was on the wrong path. She had delved into the dark arts, practising hexes and sacrificing hundreds of animals a week. Until one day, she did the unspeakable."

Alleria leant forward in her seat, her forehead wrinkling in apprehension and trepidation. "What did she do?" Her voice wobbled somewhat as she spoke.

Rosa stopped for a moment, taking the time to let her mind wander to other things. It was a dark subject, and Rosa very much believed it to all be true. "She killed a child… her own sister."

Mouth agape, Alleria sat back. How could a person do something so unthinkable to someone so young and innocent? And her sister at that? They sat in silence for a moment until Alleria remembered she had little time with Rosa. "So I will go up against a dark sorcerer?"

"You wish," she said. Alleria guessed it was her idea of a joke, but Alleria did not laugh. "The Light is very strict with its ways, and the murder of an innocent child is one of the worst offences one can commit. She was tried that day and sentenced to death by fire."

EVERYTHING JUST FELT COLD. THE IRONY OF IT ALL. Alleria swore she could feel the air condense around her. She tugged the sleeves of her shirt as far as they could go and waited for Rosa to continue, her eyes widened.

"When the pyre was lit, and Naesaela began to burn, she chanted. It was a foreign tongue no citizen in Aralva recognised. The words melded together as she quickened her speech, and then the fire changed. It moved when she did. It cried when she did. It breathed when she did. She was one with the element we all fear. The thing that could burn Aralva to the ground."

"I saw Aralva burning in my dream." Alleria blurted. The signs were all there.

Rosa inclined her head. "There is one more thing." She dropped her gaze to her lap, evading direct eye contact with Alleria. "Before they trapped her inside the mountain, she *changed*. The fire that once enveloped her now became her. One moment, she was but a girl, the next… a beast. A beast with dark stricken wings and eyes of amaranthine. She had become what you may know as a dragon."

The room fell silent as Alleria processed her words. It couldn't be… surely, dragons couldn't even exist. It was madness. The world felt like it was pushing in on Alleria; the pressure forced her head to pound.

Rosa careened her neck slightly to the other side of the kitchen and promptly jumped from her seat. "Potatoes are ready," she said, her voice suddenly chipper. She hopped the short distance to the boiling pot and took it off the open flame. When she spoke again, she didn't look over at Alleria. Instead, she focused on the food. "I know it's a lot to hear at once, but you did ask. And remember… this is all but a theory."

"So I'm expected to defeat a dragon... You *do* realise how ridiculous that sounds, right?"

"No one said it would be easy."

"They also didn't say I would battle a dragon that I assume is a hundred of times bigger than me."

"You won't be alone."

That fact eased the worry a little, but it did not negate the fact of the matter. She, a twenty-year-old girl, would be toe to toe with a winged beast that had killed many before and was more than happy to do it again. She missed Elorin, her home. She missed her mother. The library. Her friends.

"There is something more," Rosa said. Her tone was tentative, unsure if she should even mutter the words. "But you'll have to wait for Alnor, for it is his secret to tell. But I am certain he will, don't you worry."

• • •

THE FOOD WENT DOWN LIKE A TREAT, SO MUCH SO, Rosa delivered some to the neighbours.

"You must cook more often," she said to Alleria.

Alleria smiled a crookedly. Her mother loved cooking. It was an escape for her. She would never let Alleria help and had specific ways she liked to do things. But that was Pyria.

Then, Alnor glanced at his sister, to which she nodded her insistence.

"Alleria, I must tell you what I have hidden since I left Aralva, for I believe it will be of help against Naesaela."

Alleria's head jutted up from her stew. She did not know what it ever could be, but she didn't want to wait another moment longer. "Yes?"

"Come with me."

ALLERIA TRAILED BEHIND ALNOR'S GIANT STEPS passing through the house. She didn't realise it was this extensive until they reached a door bolted at five different points and seemingly formed from an incredibly thick metal. There was no keyhole.

"I have never shown anyone what lies beyond this door," he said. Alleria could sense his reluctance. If he changed his mind, Alleria felt she would explode from her curiosity. She hated surprises, but this one was too intriguing to pass up.

"Are you ready?"

"More ready than I'll ever be."

He peered behind Alleria to Rosa. "Are you ready?"

"I am." Rosa's voice sounded like butter behind Alleria. She hadn't known she was behind her this whole time. At that moment, she wondered if in another life she was a rogue spy. She had the footwork for it. Whatever was behind the door was exceptionally dangerous, and Alleria felt better knowing there were two other people here to help if it came to it.

"Very well."

Alnor pulled each bolt free one by one until they were all unlocked. The door didn't move.

"How do you open it without a key?" Alleria asked. But she was not expecting what happened next. Alnor placed his hand upon the steel door. Alleria's mouth gaped as the door disintegrated beneath his touch. Soon, the door was but a memory. A mirage she might as well have made up, for no one would've believed her.

Alnor raised his hand into the light. His once

dark brown complexion was now grey, and his hand composed of steel.

"HOW DID YOU—"

"I can absorb materials," he said casually. "It was the safest, and most secure way, to keep this locked away." He didn't note Alleria's shock at his power.

"Why didn't you tell me you could do that?" She asked.

"You didn't ask." Alnor stepped aside and let Alleria enter first. She stepped forward hesitantly, eyeing Alnor to make sure it was safe. He nodded, and she entered the dark expanse that lay before her. She careened through the dark for a few moments, scared she would trip or bump into something, until it was no longer dark. Lanterns of fire lined the stone walls and seemingly stretched for miles. How did this fit under the house?

"What is this place?" She asked as Rosa, and eventually, Alnor, appeared through the curious dark cloud that masked the *place*. Whatever was down here required so much security, it made Alleria's toes curl in fear… and doubt.

"It was formerly a dungeon, but I don't like that word," he said softly. His voice was so low,

Alleria could barely hear him. Strange, given the immense echoes whenever a slight sound was made. "I like to call it the menagerie."

"The menagerie," Alleria repeated.

"You got it!"

Alleria rolled her eyes. "Is a menagerie not a home for animals?"

Alnor craned his neck, shrugged, and turned his back to her. "You'll just have to wait and see. Come with me," he said, finally leading her down the lengthy stretch. "The cellar stretches over most of Innai."

That explains the size, Alleria thought, her gaze not leaving the brick walls as they passed through the ostensibly endless underground. It must have been centuries old, for Alleria didn't recognise the type of brickwork. Layered cobwebs littered the menagerie: a testament to its lack of use. Or was it what Rosa and Alnor wanted her to think? If something was so dusty and seemingly abandoned, it would definitely fool people. By the Light, if it wasn't for Alnor, Alleria wouldn't have thought about coming down here.

EVENTUALLY, THEY ARRIVED AT ANOTHER DOOR composed of the same material as the other. It bore the same bolts and probably the same magic but was five times the size. Alnor repeated the process from before until the door was no more. This time Alnor did not step aside to let her through. Instead, he only adjusted his head so she could see. He undoubtedly didn't trust Alleria to be in there. Or did he not trust what was in there with Alleria?

It took a long moment for Alleria's eyes to adjust, but when they did, she faltered back, a wobble in her step. She thought her eyes were deceiving her, that it was just a trick of the imagination. But no, she slept well last night, and she was fully awake. A pair of enormous emerald eyes stared back at her. She knew she wasn't seeing things, but she pinched herself to be sure, wincing at the pain. She could not believe it.

A beast.

CHAPTER 16

"Any good?"

Aiwen sipped the river water from the reservoir he formed with his palms. He pressed his lips together before spitting the water back out.

"I'm going to take that as a no," Tanyth said, his cheeks already flushed from laughing.

Once Aiwen rid his mouth of the unexpectedly salty water, he let out a chuckle of his own. As much as he annoyed him from time to time, Tanyth made the constant travelling bearable. He always found a way to make Aiwen laugh, which, in turn, made him fall in love with him even more.

• • •

"DON'T DRINK THE WATER," AIWEN SAID. "IT'S FINE for cooling down, though."

"Noted." Tanyth flicked his wrist in a mocking salute. "How long do you think we've been walking?"

"Five minutes longer than the last time you asked me," Aiwen replied. He knew Tanyth didn't have the greatest attention span, but he would be lying if he said it didn't annoy him a teeny bit. "But seriously? Your guess is as good as mine."

"It just feels like we've been walking for hours."

"Well, we have."

"I know," Tanyth said. "But surely the sun should have begun to set by now. It doesn't even seem like it's moved position in hours."

Aiwen looked to the sky. He hadn't thought about it properly, but Tanyth was right. The sun still shone brilliantly from the midday position.

"I don't like this," he remarked, his guard suddenly up. He reached behind to make sure his bow was readily accessible. When he felt the smooth curve of the wooden bow, he felt his troubles ease slightly. He and his bow almost felt like one. After years of training and time with the weapon, it hurt to be apart. Strange as it sounded in his head, he always felt more comfortable when he had it with him.

"I don't get it," Tanyth said. His gaze ricocheted around the open terrain in an attempt to identify anything out of the ordinary. He felt his chest tighten. He was sure something was watching them. "Do you feel that too, Ai?"

"I do," Aiwen retrieved his bow from his back and an arrow from his quiver. Tanyth also armed himself with his axe. "Be cautious. At any moment—"

DARKNESS REPLACED THE BLAZING MALMARIAN day. As did the looming presence. It was all but an illusion. A trick. But for what reason?

"What the fuck?" Aiwen glanced at the moon, following its light to the water beside him. It wasn't the river. It was the ocean. "Well, this explains why it was so salty."

"If we're at the ocean, that means…." Tanyth's voice trailed off.

"We were led in the wrong direction."

"But how… who—"

"Who do you think?" Aiwen interrupted. He didn't hide his frustration, but neither did Tanyth. The day had been a waste. They were even further than before.

"Do you really think Naesaela is strong enough to create a deception so *extensive*?"

"It seems so."

"It lasted for so long." Tanyth let his feet fall from beneath him until he was lying on the cold floor. "Why?"

It wasn't a question. It was a plea. His tone was suffocating in desperation. He was tired. Angry. Annoyed. Sad. Alone. Homesick. But above all, he wanted Alleria back. They both did.

"If we can look at the bright side of things," Aiwen said, sensing Tanyth gawking at him without even shifting his head. "This shows Naesaela sees us as a threat."

"How so?" It was a genuine question.

"Why else trick us in the opposite direction?" Aiwen's voice raised as the puzzle pieces fell into place in his head. "Naesaela realises how much family drives Alleria. How she would feel stronger and safer with us around—"

"Naesaela is intimidated."

"I don't think it's that," Aiwen corrected. "She isn't ready. She's delaying Alleria as much as possible for the mountain to break completely."

"I think you're right." Tanyth sat up, his face still glazed in worry. "Where do we go from here now?"

"Well, we must be on the west side of Malmar.

There is no possible way we could have travelled all the way east in the time we were walking. Besides, it's all forest." Aiwen crouched and let his fingers dance upon the rippling waters as if it would tell him where they were. "Innai is roughly northeast of here."

"We must set off immediately," Tanyth said. "I can't sleep knowing this."

"Of course, but we must also hope Alleria has already deduced what we have. If she is still in Innai when Naesaela breaks free," Aiwen swallowed hard. "I don't want to think about what would happen."

"Time is running out quicker than we thought."

❄

"IS THAT WHAT I THINK IT IS?"

"Well, what *do* you think it is?"

Alleria rolled her eyes. She wanted to step forward to get a better look, but her feet wouldn't allow it. She felt like she was glued to the floor, and, in a way, she was thankful for it. From what she knows from the myths, dragons are unpredictable and highly wary. If they stepped too close, they could be ash on the floor in seconds. And this would have all been for nothing.

"How did you get a dragon in here?" Alleria asked, her eyes fixated on the creature in front of her. It's hadn't blinked once. Any creature that didn't blink would be unnerving, but the dragon's scale just added to the terror.

Alnor didn't answer right away. Instead, he chuckled. Alleria did not know why, but he was awfully loud. She jutted her eye-line from Alnor to the creature to be sure his obnoxious guffaws did not disturb it.

"Relax, Alleria. He is well trained." As he strode forward and knelt beside the dragon's head, it did the unthinkable. The dragon nestled into Alnor, and Alnor allowed it. No fear permeated his dark eyes. It seemed as if this was an everyday activity for him.

"This is Vaalyun," he said endearingly. "And he is not a dragon. Vaalyun is a hippogriff."

"A hippogriff?" Alleria could not hide her confusion. "Are you sure?"

"Yes, I am sure. Look, come here." He tapped the spot next to him, ushering her to join him.

Alleria looked to Rosa; she bowed her head, noticing Alleria's internal queries.

"I've been in here hundreds of times. You'll be

perfectly fine." She nudged Alleria slightly forward.

After much internal deliberation, Alleria bit her lip, took a deep breath, and tiptoed into the room. It was dark and damp, but as she walked further in, the creature became more visible. The light, from what she assumed to be the outside, highlighted it perfectly. Now that she thought about it, maybe some magic was in play. She didn't know how far underground they were; light might not be able to reach this far down. Feathers covered the creature's entire frame, something she hadn't seen from where she stood in the door.

"BY THE WAY, I DID NOT SEE ITS FEATHERS FROM over there," Alleria said, fighting the embarrassment of mistaking a hippogriff, a half eagle, half horse, for a dragon. "He is exquisite, though."

"Sure... give him a pat," Alnor said. He withdrew his hand from Vaalyun's neck for Alleria to test the waters. "I'm sure you have a lot of questions."

"That is the understatement of the century," Alleria muttered, reaching over to stroke the hippogriff. When her fingers finally came in contact with the creature, she almost gasped. The feathers were softer than anything she'd ever felt. Vaalyun almost purred as her petting quickened, to which Alnor chuckled.

"As you can see, Vaalyun is as gentle as a creature can get." He climbed to his feet and waltzed to a door on the other side of the room. Alleria hadn't noticed it until now. "He's more like a common canine than a mythical creature, really." The door was not locked like the others they passed through. All he did was push it back. Behind, lay a horde of meats and other foods.

ALLERIA STRUGGLED TO KEEP VAALYUN DOWN WHEN he eventually caught sight of his meals. One moment he was resting beside her, the next, he was squawking for nourishment. Now he stood. Alleria could thoroughly inspect the creature she thought was a myth mere minutes ago. As her gaze wandered down its spine, the feathers dispersed into a silky fur. All Alleria could think about was how fast Vaalyun might be able to fly. His wings weren't stretched out, but she could tell the wingspan was impressive.

"You have already eaten today," Alnor said. "You can have one more piece of meat since you've been so good with Alleria." He pulled a piece of what looked like beef from the stacked shelves and threw it towards Vaalyun. Effortlessly, he caught it in his mouth and swallowed it in one.

"He's absolutely incredible," Alleria said. "How—why is he down here?"

Alnor shut the door behind him. He patted Vaalyun's feathered head and ambled toward Alleria. "Malmar isn't safe for his kind anymore."

"How so?"

"It's a long story—"

"I have some time."

Alnor looked at Rosa before giving in. "Very well."

ALLERIA FOLLOWED ALNOR OUT OF THE ROOM, BUT not before stroking Vaalyun one last time. He attempted to nestle into her chest, and it broke her heart to leave him alone. What a remarkable creature.

"What are we doing out here?" Alleria asked.

"See all these doors?" He pointed down the long hall. Every few lengths, another thick metal door disrupted the brick walls.

"I do."

"Behind each door, more creatures lie."

Alleria's eyes widened. "You mean to tell me, Vaalyun isn't the only one?"

"He isn't the only one, no," He said. Alleria could tell he'd never done this before. He was uncomfortable sharing this secret. "He's also not the *only* creature."

"Not just hippogriffs?"

"No."

Alleria didn't know how long they looked through doors and marvelled at the creatures that lied behind them. Creatures of the past, creatures that weren't supposed to exist. All alive and well. Gryphon. Basilisk. Chimaera. All of them.

"I think that is enough for today," Alnor spoke, bolting the door behind him. "You get the point, right?"

Alleria nodded her head, but she still didn't know why they were here. "Why?"

"Why what?"

"Why are they down here?"

"It is my job," he said. "Well, it was my job in Aralva—"

"Why don't we go talk about this upstairs," Rosa interrupted. Her arms hugged herself to keep warm. Alleria only just realised she was cold, too. "Alnor, I think you forget this is technically a dungeon. We'll catch a death if we're here for any longer."

• • •

TEN MINUTES LATER, THEY WERE ALL STRETCHED OUT on armchairs in the living room. The fireplace exhumed a needed warmth, yet Rosa still had wrapped herself in a blanket.

"As I was saying before I was ever so rudely interrupted," Alnor finally said. He laughed at Rosa's joking glare. "In Aralva, I was the owner of the menagerie. I looked after the creatures that would, without my help, terrorise Malmar for food."

"I'm still confused," Alleria stated. She sipped her piping tea Rosa had made minutes before. "Why are they here? Why not keep them in Aralva, where they're better guarded."

"I'm selfish, I suppose. I didn't trust anyone else in Aralva to take care of them. But I didn't trust anyone else to make sure they were well fed, whilst also making sure they don't wreak."

Alleria could see the love he had for the creatures. She didn't know if Alnor had children, but his animals seemed to be the closest thing.

"I think they have a good life with me," he continued. "They just don't get to stretch their wings or run around the fields like they could in Aralva." Alnor dropped his head, his heart aching for the creatures.

"I'm sure they have a glorious life," Alleria confirmed, not wanting Alnor to be even more dismayed. "They're intelligent creatures. They know you have their best intentions in mind."

"Exactly," Rosa said. "You're wonderful with them. You know that."

Alnor sniffled.

"So, all the mythical creatures are down there?" Alleria asked, truly curious. How long did it take to transfer them?

"Only the ones that can't communicate in a spoken language. Humanoid creatures like minotaurs and centaurs reside in Aralva."

"That's incredible." Alleria was still trying to wrap her head around the fact that all these things existed in the same universe as her, let alone in the same proximity. "I have to ask, why did you show me Vaalyun first?"

Alnor shifted in his seat like he'd waited for her to ask. "Vaalyun is very devoted and loyal. I think he'd be immensely helpful in your battle against Naesaela."

"You want me to take a hippogriff to battle?"

"Indeed."

"I couldn't," Alleria said. "I couldn't bear to see him injured."

"Do not let his soft exterior fool you. Vaalyun

is a vicious and monstrous creature when he needs to be."

Alleria sipped her tea once again, her mind spiralling as she did so. She thought of Vaalyun, and how there was no possibility the loving ball of fur could be harmful. That was until she remembered his intimidating presence. Her world had already been turned upside down, and she felt it was about to again. She couldn't keep up with her surroundings. It pained her to keep adjusting her life, but she had to. Malmar depended on her. She would have time to work on herself once everyone was safe. Then, she realised, so much had happened. She hadn't thought of her mother for days. Maybe it was a blessing in disguise to keep going, if not for Malmar, for her mother.

"Very well, what is your plan?"

CHAPTER 17

Darkness still shrouded Malmar as Tanyth and Aiwen trekked closer and closer to Innai. They had trudged along the ocean, and when it felt right, they would turn east to reach the village. Aiwen said it would be easier to spot anything out of the ordinary if we didn't have to worry about things from every direction. Tanyth agreed it was a lot less likely for something to attack from the ocean. Though, not impossible.

"YOU STILL THERE?" AIWEN ASKED.

"Yes." Tanyth was lugging behind, fighting his flickering eyelids. He tried to slap himself awake multiple times, but it wasn't working anymore. Sleep was imminent. "As much as I want to keep going, I don't know how much longer I can stay awake."

"Just a little further," Aiwen said sympathetically. He stopped in his tracks and waited for Tanyth to catch up. When he did, he wrapped his left arm around his shoulder and pulled him close. "Do it for me, and I'll reward you."

Tanyth chuckled. "I'm so tired that a promise of a kiss does not excite me, Ai."

"Do it for Alleria then."

"Is this not what this is all about, anyway?"

"Of course, it is."

"Then why say it like I don't know that?"

"Tanyth." Aiwen blinked his eyes, startled at his sudden outburst. "What is wrong?"

"I'm sorry," he finally said. "I'm just so stressed. And worried. And—"

"I know you are, and that's ok. I'd be concerned if you weren't."

Tanyth kissed him on the cheek. "Thank you."

"We will walk to the end of this dune. If there's nothing out of the ordinary, we'll set up camp there."

"I can agree with that," Tanyth said. Despite his lack of sleep, he still looked perfect. His blond curls were still coiled. His blue eyes were a complementary shade to the ocean that rippled next to them.

NOT LONG AFTERWARD, THEY CLAMBERED UP THE final sandy dune.

"The moment of truth," Aiwen said, right as his head peeked over the hill. "Holy shit."

"What?" Tanyth was mere steps behind, but when he captured a glimpse of what shocked Aiwen, Tanyth gasped in excitement.

"What village is this?"

"I have no idea."

"It's not Innai, is it?"

"No, Innai is on the river."

"Well, this is better than sleeping on the floor again."

"That is if they have any spare rooms."

Aiwen stepped closer, his hand in Tanyth's. As they reached the gates of the village, he ripped his grasp away.

Tanyth eyed him.

"We don't know how these people might react," Aiwen explained. He had always been apprehensive about that fact, but luckily, the people of Elorin did not care.

"But—"

"Look, Tanyth," His hands were on his

shoulders, their heads rested against each other. "We need a room. I just don't want to ruin our chances."

"Ruin? We shouldn't have to hide who we are."

"We're not hiding who we are," Aiwen said firmly. "We're merely not telling them."

"I don't know…."

"Tanyth, I love you, and that is all that matters."

He reached in, grazed his cheek with his fingertips, and before pulling away, whispered in his ear. "Besides, secrets are fun."

Tanyth beamed. "Who are you, and what have you done with my boyfriend?"

"Oh, are we boyfriends?"

"Well, you just said you loved me," Tanyth said casually. "I think they go hand in hand, right?"

Aiwen giggled. "Very well, boyfriend. Let's find a room."

❄

"ARE YOU NOT COMING WITH US?" ALLERIA SAID whilst turning to leave the house. In her peripheral, she noticed Rosa was still seated.

Rosa shifted in her seat. "I'm going to stay

here and look after the…." Her voice trailed off, but Alleria knew what she was referring to. "Besides, I'm not one for a battle. I don't have a useful power like Alnor, and I never received proper training. I'd be more of an interference than anything."

Alleria strode over to Rosa, not caring that Alnor was probably outside awaiting her presence. She perched on the side of the armchair. "You stay safe," she said as she embraced her in a mighty hug. "I hope to see you again one day."

"You're welcome anytime, Alleria," she said. "It's been lovely to get to know you. Your mother would have been so proud."

"Thank you. That means a lot. Also, if Aiwen and Tanyth make it to Innai, please inform them I'm on my way to Aralva."

Pyria nodded and placed a farewell kiss on Alleria's forehead and rushed her away. "Of course. Now, quick before he gets snappy."

Alleria chuckled. She drew herself away from Rosa and stalked to the front door once again.

Closing the door behind her, it hit her how important she really was, as conceited as that sounded. If she didn't fulfil her prophecy and destroy Naesaela for good, she would be to blame for these innocent people's brutal murders. Including Rosa. As she raced toward the riverside, where she trained earlier that morning, she didn't let her gaze linger on the few people left in the streets.

They didn't know it, but she was their only hope. A lump of fear congealed in her throat, but she pushed it down in an instant. She wouldn't let her feelings cloud her judgement, not when everyone depended on her. Now, she just hoped Alnor's plan would work.

When she finally arrived at the riverside, Alnor wasn't the first thing she saw. Her eyes went straight to the two hippogriffs behind him. She knew one of them was Vaalyun, but the other was a mystery to her. It was a similar shade but had a stripe of red feathers down its back. It was truly fascinating.

"Who's this beauty?" Alleria asked, dropping her bag to the floor so she could take a better look. She brushed her hands through its feathery mane as it purred like Vaalyun did just a few hours ago.

"I see she has taken a liking to you already," Alnor said, his voice threaded with astonishment. "She's female, and they don't tend to get along with other female… creatures."

"Are you calling me a creature, Alnor?" Alleria arched her brow.

"We're all animals, Alleria," he said, shrugging. "Humans just colonised the world before any other could."

"I don't know how true that statement is, but I won't dispute it."

"History wasn't my strong suit, so you're probably right. But the sentiment is there," Alnor said. She stroked Vaalyun's neck. Alleria could sense Vaalyun's jealousy Alnor probably did too. "Her name is Nephinae. I figured I ought to bring her along."

"Nephinae," Alleria repeated. She couldn't take her eyes off the creature, still in disbelief that she had resided in Malmar for twenty years, not knowing creatures like this actually existed. Nephinae stared back at her before leaning in to show her affection. "I assume I'll be taking her?"

"I think she's making sure of that," Alnor said. "It seems she's chosen you."

"Hippogriffs choose their riders?"

"Yes, and no. They will let most people ride them, but they have to *choose* you to let you do it again."

"So they only let a person ride once if they're not chosen?"

"More or less. It is more so because of

emergency situations. In the past, hippogriffs have suffered tremendous neglect. They know how it feels to be in a situation where you need to escape."

Alleria raised her brow. "That is awful, but also incredibly intelligent."

"It has also been said that hippogriffs can sense a person's true intentions," he added. "That is how they *choose*."

TO NEPHINAE'S DISMAY, ALLERIA FINALLY STEPPED away. She swept the dirt from her breeches and retrieved her bag from the floor.

"You're eager," Alnor said, still fussing over Vaalyun and Nephinae. She leaned into him, wanting to be pet as well. It made Alleria chuckle at how faithful these animals were. Who would have thought?

"I think the longer we wait, the more chance Naesaela has to…." Alleria didn't want to finish that sentence. She wasn't highly superstitious, but she didn't want to put the words out there if they somehow manifested themselves into existence. It seemed ridiculous, even impossible, but stranger things have happened. It wasn't worth the risk.

"Smart girl," he said. His face suddenly

stretched upward as if he recalled something significant. "The town crier came to me earlier today. I completely forgot to tell you. That is my fault… But there have been reports across Malmar of abnormal *activity*."

"How so?" Alleria wanted to laugh at the fact. Of course, they couldn't just have an ordinary day. Something had to go wrong. It shouldn't be surprising to her anymore.

"More of those possessions you told us of and… time illusions."

Alleria's confused face alone told Alnor he needed to go into detail. He did. "I'm not so sure myself, if I'm truly honest. However, there are reports near to the forest of Malmar of halted daylight."

"I'm sorry?" Alleria couldn't wrap her head around it.

"It seems something, or someone, made it appear like it was a day for a lot longer than it was."

"Is the illusion still active?"

"No," he said. "It vanished. The people around those parts were very perplexed when the bright sky suddenly just darkened. Some even said they were in a different place to where they thought they were." Alnor snorted. "There is no easy way to explain this, is there?"

"I think I understand now," Alleria said. "Do you think it was Naesaela?"

"I assume so, it's dark magic… You haven't had your nightmares or any visions recently, have you?"

Alleria shook her head.

"Maybe this is why."

"It makes little sense," she said. Naesaela was smart. She wouldn't be using her limited magic source unless imperative. "Why waste her magic on an illusion like that?"

"I think Naesaela wants us to question that and give her more time to build up strength."

Alleria sighed. "You're right. I'm sure it's nothing. A mere deterrence, if anything."

STILL DISSATISFIED, ALLERIA PREPPED NEPHINAE FOR flight. The whole time, her thoughts ran circles inside her head. She couldn't come up with a logical explanation for Naesaela's actions. There had to be a reason for it. Unless…

"Where were the reports again?"

Alnor stopped brushing Vaalyun. "By the forest—"

"I know what she was doing," Alleria said. How could she be so blind? "My friends. She was trying to stop them from reaching me. It must be them." Her chest tightened at the thought.

"I'm sure they are ok, Alleria."

Alleria nodded, though she was unsure herself. They were strong men, but she still worried. At least, she had confirmation one of them survived their encounter with the wolf. That fact made the knot forming in Alleria's stomach loosen. She still didn't know where they were now and whether Naesaela succeeded in tricking them. But she had faith.

"Alleria." Alnor's voice boomed through her mental prison. He must have been trying to get through to her for a few moments. "Are you alright?"

"Yes, sorry."

Alnor eyed her, knowing that wasn't the case. He didn't ask again, which Alleria was grateful for. Talking about it might make it worse.

"Now... Nephinae should stay right behind Vaalyun. If, for some reason, you lose us, carry on north. Fly until you see the river split into two. We will land on a small desert between the river and Aralva. Then we should be able to walk through the border."

"I thought it was just all green valleys around Aralva?"

"The desert is right before it. Unwanted

travellers only ever see the desert. When they try to enter—well, it doesn't matter."

"But my friends—"

"You will be there to escort them in," he interrupted. "Alleria, you mustn't worry from now on. You need to have a clear mind."

Alleria hung her head in defeat. He was right, but it wasn't like she could just switch off her humanity. Then, she wondered if there was a creature that could. Indeed, there must be. There were hundreds of doors in the menagerie, full of incredible species, and there were even more in Aralva that she couldn't wait to see.

Alnor climbed onto Vaalyun and ushered Alleria to mount Nephinae. She patted her back, prompting the creature to lower her body for her to hop on. Alleria whispered her thanks and clambered on. It felt no different to riding Blanchy. She did hope Blanchy was alive, but that was wishful thinking. If only the mare had stayed with the group, she could've had some feathered friends to live out her days. But she understood. She was scared. Alleria knew the feeling all too well.

VAALYUN AND NEPHINAE STOOD SIDE BY SIDE, THEIR gaze focused north. Alleria and Alnor's conversation going over the plan once again didn't seem to disturb them. They were calm, which was surprising considering it was their first time out of the menagerie in twenty years. The hippogriffs must have been aching to stretch their wings and feel the air pass through their feathers. Alleria couldn't wait to see the world from their point of view. She loved to marvel at nature, and she could only imagine how beautiful it must be from above.

"That seems to be all," Alnor said. "Do you need me to run it over once more?"

Alleria laughed. "No, I understand."

"Very well, hold tight to Nephinae. From what I remember, she's a brave flyer."

TO ALLERIA'S UTTER SURPRISE, NEPHINAE MOVED first. She began to trot, and then she ran. Already, Alleria's hair was blowing behind her, and she wished she tied it up. By the time they reached Aralva, it would look more like a bee-hive than hair. Her gaze drifted to Alnor, his locks stationary on his head, the heft weighing them down. When he caught her gaze, he smirked at what she could only assume was her hair. Surely, it wasn't that bad—

Nephinae lifted from the floor, forcing Alleria

to wrap her arms tighter around her girthy neck. The feathers tickled her arms, but she soon got used to it. They soared higher and higher until Innai was practically toy village. It was quite beautiful, really.

Despite the winds, she fought the urge to clamp her eyes shut, wanting to take in every moment. The bright dawn light cracked through the clouds, momentarily disorientating her. She hadn't realised they had been awake the entire night. But all she could think about was her past. She missed her friends and her mother. And her job. She missed her life.

CHAPTER 18

The streets were desolate, and the night was swiftly waning. They crossed through the sleeping village until they reached a narrow terraced building. It was quaint but exuded a certain charm. The sign on the front read *'The Maid's Inn.'*

"Do you think it's an inn?" Tanyth asked.

"I hope you're joking." Aiwen nudged him and lazily opened the door.

IT WAS A SMALL ENTRYWAY, STREWED WITH BOOKS OF old and new, lit with large candelabras on every flat surface possible. The wax had overflown the plates below them, seeping onto the cold wooden floor. They must have been lit a long while ago. It added a certain character to the room. they must have been lit a long while ago. A woman, no older than forty, sat behind a desk on the opposite side of the room. Her brows lifted when she spotted Tanyth and Aiwen enter.

"Well, well," she said. Her voice was scratchy, almost as if she had just woken up. She probably had. It was only just turning into morning. "Who do we have here?"

Aiwen spoke first, knowing Tanyth would probably say too much, "Hello, my friend and I are looking for a room for the night—well, day."

"Have you and your... friend come a great way?" She transferred her gaze from the boys to the large open book in front of her. She flipped the pages before settling on a page seemingly full to the brim of names.

"Yes, we just need some time to rest before we leave again."

She nodded her head. "Where are you heading?"

Tanyth went to open his mouth but froze after Aiwen kicked him in the leg.

"Nowhere in particular," Aiwen said. "We just like to travel." His voice had no conviction, but it was the best he could do at the moment. Tanyth's love for oversharing shouldn't surprise him anymore.

The woman furrowed her brow but didn't ask any further questions. "Room thirteen, up the stairs. Payment on exit." She held up a large, rusted key that, years ago, might have been gilded.

Aiwen reached over and took it from her hand. "Thank you very much…" Aiwen said, waiting for her name.

"Jessamine."

"It's lovely to meet you, Jessamine. I'm Aiwen, and this is Tanyth."

WHEN AIWEN FINALLY UNLOCKED THE DOOR, THEY both stepped in. One enormous bed greeted them. Aiwen was about to comment on it, but Tanyth spoke first.

"What happened to being discreet?"

Aiwen craned his neck toward his lover. "What do you mean?"

"You just told her our real names."

Aiwen went to speak but stopped, his mouth agape. "I didn't think."

"Obviously." Tanyth rolled his eyes. He stepped further into the room, admiring the minimal decoration, before jumping onto the bed. Elorin was so small, everything was cluttered. It was nice to enter a room that wasn't stacked with knick knacks and other useless decoration. He moaned when his head cemented itself on the soft, cushioned surface. “Well, by the looks of this bed, she knew we were together. And guess what… she didn’t care. I told you.”

“Look, Tanyth. I’m sorry about before.” He lay down beside him on the bed, his face inches away from his. “I’m still new to this.”

“We’re both new to this,” Tanyth corrected.

“Yes, of course, but,” Aiwen’s voice quickened as his words blurred together. “I do not know how to deal with these feelings and I do not like being judged and I get so nervous when I meet new people and I want to make a good impression—”

TANYTH LUNGED FORWARD AND PLACED HIS MOUTH on Aiwen’s. He leaned in, revelling in the intimacy, before pulling away. Short but sweet.

“What was that for?” he said, flustered. Sweat had beaded his lip. “Is that the only way you know how to calm me?”

“You needed a distraction… so I gave you one. Besides, it always works.” Tanyth’s lips curved upward. It wasn’t a lie.

“But—”

“Your feelings are valid, and I understand

why you get so nervous. It's perfectly natural," Tanyth said, reassuring him. "But when you're with me, I'm going to do everything in my power to make you feel safe and respected because you…."

"Because what?"

Tanyth gave a genuine smile. Little dimples formed around his mouth, something Aiwen had never really noticed before. It added even more to his beauty. "You are the most incredible person I've ever met, and I've never loved someone like I love you."

"Tanyth, you were with countless people before me."

"But I didn't love them," he continued. "I thought I did. I thought I knew what love was. But I was wrong." He leaned in once again until his forehead rested against Aiwen's, and their noses caressed each other. "Love is when you feel safe, and when you feel you can tell them everything and not be afraid to leave out any details. My love was amiss, twisted in misguided tethers, bound by a false truth. Aiwen, love is when I'm with you."

TANYTH CLOSED THE SHORT DISTANCE BETWEEN them and let their lips collide. It seemed their displays of affection always occurred like this. Unexpected, and when they really needed it. Again, it felt like the first time. They could almost feel the sparks bursting out of them. Moments passed, and they clung together, each of them unable to pull away.

"I don't want to let go," Aiwen said between kisses. His eyes focused on Tanyth's. He could drown in his cobalt blue, and he wouldn't mind. He was lost in a maze of love, and he hoped he wouldn't find the exit. But he would be lying if the maze didn't feel like a trap from time to time. Like the walls were just a little too high—

Tanyth kept his lips still but didn't move them away. They were still for a moment before he spoke. His voice oozing with truth and lust. "Then don't."

❄

THE WIND WAS THE BEST DISTRACTION. IT BLASTED into Alleria, slamming her troubles away. She had more serious issues to deal with, but this was a needed and deserved distraction. She still clung on for dear life, her arms latched around Nephinae's neck, but Alnor seemed to have no issue. He oozed grace when he flew, his eyes full of determination and no strain showed on his face.

The wind didn't even seem to trouble him. He was in his element, despite the inability to practise for two decades. He disappeared and reappeared through the clouds over and over until he pointed down. They had flown too high and couldn't see the land.

Alleria leant forward, hoping Nephinae would listen. The thought of losing Alnor mid-flight did not sound ideal.

Suddenly, the hippogriff plunged downward. Alleria's arms ached from holding on so tight, but adrenaline soon kicked in. She stiffened her legs around Nephinae's body and planted her head into the animal's feathers, her eyes shut. The wind slammed even harder against her body now, like it was pleading for her to let go. For dear life, she dug her fingers into the creature's side, hoping she didn't mind.

Then, whispers of the wind caressed her face. It was gentle, tender. The dreaded feeling of falling had gone. Reluctantly, she opened her eyes. They took a moment to readjust, but Nephinae was not far off the ground, just above a lake or a river. She couldn't tell. She spotted Alnor, just across from her, clutching his head.

His descent must not have been smooth, either. They were at a standstill, yet still in the air.

"Nephinae," Alnor said. His voice barely cut through the soft gales. It was as if the wind wanted to dampen his commands and wanted for Alleria to fail. "You went too low. We need to go up again." With that, Alnor and Vaalyun disappeared into the sky before settling just below the clouds.

SHE SWORE SHE HEARD ANOTHER YELL, BUT IT WAS almost inaudible from where she was. She leaned into Nephinae's body once again, whispering her commands to the creature. Nephinae did not move. Instead, she floated in the same spot, watching the clouds pass.

"Please, Nephinae," Alleria pleaded. She danced her hands through her feathers, hoping to entice her. "If I don't reach Aralva, everyone will die." Nothing. Alleria didn't know what to do, Nephinae needed a reason. "Including, Alnor."

Nephinae surged upward.

INITIALLY, A SMILE BROKE FROM ALLERIA'S FACE, but she soon realised her grip was not enough. Her fingers slid through the hippogriff's feathers, and her body free fell. She swung her arms frantically around, attempting to latch onto anything, to no avail.

Panic soared through her veins. She felt the air crashing around her. Her helpless body tumbled through clouds, catapulting through the sky toward the ground below. She did not expect to fall so unexpectedly. Just like the breaking of a promise, it pulled at her wings until there was nothing left, leaving her to crash and burn, without a warning.

No sound would, or could, leave her mouth. She couldn't bring herself to scream. Every time she opened her mouth to do so, the sweet but terrifying allure of death suffocated her. Instead, her cries for help were internal. The saviour of Malmar, killed by falling. That would be the story. Her prophecy failed because of her own incompetence. She should have held on tighter or spoken gentler. In her last moments, she let her eyes rest and did not open them again until she hit the ground.

CHAPTER 19

The water of the lake below invaded Alleria wherever it could. On impact with the surface, she passed out. Her body sank further with every fleeting moment. Had Nephinae even noticed Alleria was gone?

The light of day cascaded into the lake illuminating Alleria's location. With a jolt, Alleria's eyes shot open. She sunk to the depths of water. She could see silhouettes of the two hippogriffs flying above, unknowing of where Alleria lay. Her body slumped to the ground, and she fought every voice inside her, telling her to let go. She had the urge to cough, but she knew letting more water invade her was a death wish.

The daylight shone brighter, straining her eyesight. It seemed to grow before her. Until she was *in* the Light. It was not daylight after all. Suddenly, her body lurched upward being dragged to the surface. A barrier between herself and water had formed, and she could breathe again. She triumphed in the air that clogged her lungs and took no time in coughing up the water that had ravaged her insides.

The silhouettes grew closer and closer until Alnor appeared. His frame crashed through the water, swimming downward with his eyes closed and his skin glittering. It was changing before her; absorbing the water that encased him. But when he his eyes searched for Alleria, he couldn't contain his shock. In awe, he watched as the Light lifted Alleria. Realising she required no further help, he swam upward again, and they both resurfaced simultaneously.

"Alleria, are you ok?" He waded to where she was floating above the water. Then, the light faded, and she was swimming by herself. She trod water to keep afloat. Alnor held her body in his and flapped his hand in the air. His being returned to its original state, like he had not been one with the water. Suddenly, Nephinae swooped down. Alleria ought to be angry at the creature, but she could detect the sadness in her eyes. The creature had been locked up for two decades and was simply over excited. Alleria couldn't stay mad at that. Nephinae submerged herself in the lake water and let Alnor place Alleria back on her back.

"I have already told Nephinae of her mistakes," he spoke. "She won't do it again. Maybe it is best if we travel by land for the rest of the journey?"

Alleria shook her head in defiance. "No, there's not enough time."

"Alleria—"

"No, Alnor," Alleria interrupted. "Nephinae will just be more careful this time, right?" Alleria inclined her head toward Nephinae. The animal bowed her head, agreeing with Alleria's queries. She turned back to Alnor, who was sceptical. "See!"

Her persuasion seemed to have worked. "Very well. But I'm flying right by your side."

THE REST OF THE JOURNEY WAS ENJOYABLE. THEY flew just above the ground, allowing Alleria to do what she cherished most: marvel at nature. Plants of many origins littered the scenery. They passed through forests and meadows, which Alleria was most happy about. Woodlands were her safe place, and as awful as her experience in the forest was, she would be lying if she said she didn't somewhat enjoy it. She turned to Alnor, who, true to his word, was right beside her.

"Are you alright?" he said. He had to raise his voice to cut through the winds, but not enough to yell.

Alleria nodded her head. "How much further do you think it is?"

"Do you see the river?" Alleria followed his pointed finger to the river right of her. "Soon, we need to fly above it, and then eventually it will—"

"Split." Alleria finished his sentence.

"Indeed. We're going to fly straight through the desert now. No stopping… ah, here we go."

ALLERIA SHIFTED HER GAZE BACK, THE SPLIT suddenly appearing before her. It wasn't magic, just good timing. Vaalyun turned, and so did Nephinae. They flew directly towards the water until they were on top of it. Alleria could see the water rippling as the hippogriffs flew over. She noticed the sides of the river begin to curve, and when she looked back up, she saw the desert between the split. It was barren, and seemingly nothing lay upon it. But she knew that wasn't the case. From what she gathered from Alnor, it was an illusion. Not too different to the magic that shrouded the book in the library. That felt like months ago, but in reality, only a week passed. Alleria had lost track of time, and hoped this would all be over soon.

As they finally entered the desert, Alleria fought against the brewing ache in her head. Was this the deterrence Alnor spoke of? After a few moments, the pain passed, and they were soaring peacefully. Alnor did not take his eyes off of his invisible destination.

Alleria felt her body twitch in anticipation as her skin began to crawl, and her hair stood on end. She was hesitant how other people would react. Would they scold her for not coming sooner? How would they feel about Pyria's passing?

"Hold on!" Alnor yelled, making sure Alleria heard.

A rumbling sounded in her head. It wasn't painful, but it forced her to close her eyes for a moment to recover. A slight discomfort. Then, Nephinae shook. They were passing through a barrier of sorts. Alleria looked to Vaalyun, and he was struggling similarly. Suddenly, she saw it. A dome encompassed the area in front of them, and they were crossing through it, slowing them down immensely.

Glimpses of what layed inside peeked through the barrier. It was real. She could briefly see the clock tower. Alleria found herself smiling. She had indeed made the journey, sacrificing much to get here, but she hoped it was worth it. At that moment, the rumbling was no more, and Nephinae picked up her speed again.

VALLEYS OF GREEN ENVELOPED ALLERIA'S VISION. Everything from her dreams, they were real. Thankfully, it was still vibrant, unlike her nightmares. Her gaze met Alnor's, who didn't even try to hide his excitement to be back to where he was from. Technically, Alleria was from here too, but it didn't feel like it. She hoped she'd get to return to Elorin when this was all over. It was her home, it was all she ever knew. Alnor released a resounding victory cry and leaned forward for Vaalyun to land. Nephinae followed suit until they were finally back on the ground.

By the looks of it, they landed in the same spot as when Alleria first dreamed of Aralva. It was surreal feeling like something out of a children's book. If it wasn't for what she had seen this past week, Alleria never would have believed it. Her eye-line shot around her she spotted more creatures in the air. She couldn't tell what they were from her location, but she surmised they must have been incredible.

Alnor hopped off the hippogriff and ran to Alleria, wrapping his arms around her before she had a chance to stretch her legs. He beamed from ear to ear, not caring what she might think of him. In the few days, she'd known him, she never saw him so happy.

"I can't believe it," he said, his focus unable to stay on one thing for longer than a moment.

"You didn't think we'd make it?" Alleria said. She was joking, but she did not have high hopes either. She really thought she'd die in that lake. Thankfully, her clothes had dried during the rest of the flight.

"There was a moment where I was doubtful," he admitted. "But it's incredible to be back here." He jumped in joy, to which Alleria chuckled. "I can't wait to show you around. I hope they haven't changed things around too much."

"What do we do about Vaalyun and Nephinae?"

Alnor smiled. "They can do what they like," he said. "They're home."

Alike Alnor, Alleria could not hide her joy

either. It was truly the prettiest place she ever laid her eyes on. Her dream did not do the forgotten land justice. But something was different. She pondered for a moment, about to ask Alnor, when it hit her.

"Where is Mount Tejon?"

"Hidden by an ancient Elven magic," Alnor said. "I see it, right there." He pointed behind her, but when she turned nothing lay on the horizon. "An elf has to remove the glamour for each Aralven citizen. Since you've been away for so long, that glamour must have rebuilt itself."

"I see."

"No need to fret. Once we find Ayen, they'll eliminate the glamour."

Alleria nodded and arrayed her gaze on Aralva. "Shall we go?"

"I thought you'd never ask."

CHAPTER 20

Tanyth woke to a garish light, his face scorched, and his body plastered in sweat. He rubbed his tired eyes and wobbled to the open curtains. The blistering sun bared through the thin glass windows directly on the bed Aiwen still slept on. By the position of the sun, Tanyth guessed it must have been early afternoon. Squinting, he glanced over at the bustling village, a lot livelier than it was when they arrived.

He watched for a while, indulging in the masses upon masses of people that walked below. They were the first people he'd seen since leaving Elorin. He envied their ignorance to the impending ruin. He missed the time when he was in the same naïve position. As much as he loved, and would do anything for Alleria, the stress of the situation was all too much; he was just glad he didn't have any family he had left behind.

Only when a young man caught his stare did he remove himself from his prying position. He did not want to bring any more attention to himself than needed, so he drew the curtains as he walked away and reclaimed his place back in bed beside Aiwen.

He couldn't help but extend his stare, but this time, at his lover. As weird as it sounded in his head, despite the circumstances, this was the first time they'd been *away* together. Aiwen had always been wary of others' acceptance of their relationship and would decline Tanyth's invitations to travel to nearby villages.

"ARE YOU GOING TO STARE AT ME ALL DAY?" AIWEN said.

Tanyth jumped where he lay. He'd been so enthralled in his memories, he'd not noticed Aiwen's flickering eyes.

"I was just thinking," Tanyth said once he caught his breath.

Aiwen raised his brow, gesturing to know more. Just then, he realised how hot it was and snatched the damp sheets away from his body.

He arched his back upward, in an attempt to air his body, and wound back to Tanyth.

"What made you think so much you didn't even realise I had woken up?"

"Just us," Tanyth said.

"What about us?"

"Just." He ran his fingers through his blonde locks and sighed. He didn't want to get into it right now. "How good you and I look together. It's terrifying."

Aiwen smirked before climbing out of bed. "Hilarious." Tanyth didn't see Aiwen's face stoop as he turned away to dress.

DESPITE THE CROWDED STREETS, THE DOWNSTAIRS OF The Maid's Inn was virtually empty, bar Jessamine, who still remained behind the desk. As they reached the bottom of the steps, she pointed to the door next to her without a word. They nodded their thanks and stepped into a busier tavern area. It didn't look too different from the old tavern in Elorin. Tens of people, all seemingly middle-aged, sat around circular tables drinking all-sorts of ales and wines. Heads turned as they made their way through to the few empty tables left, but luckily, their gazes didn't linger.

Tanyth guided Aiwen through, wanting to grab for his hand. But knowing Aiwen would have pulled away, he didn't.

"Feels like home," Aiwen said as they parked themselves in a booth in the outer corner of the tavern.

"It does, indeed."

Before speaking further, a young dark-skinned woman with jet black hair braided to her shoulders stepped up to the table. She was gracious in the way she presented herself with a lengthy smile plastered on her face. "What can I get for you two today?" Her tone lofty and as striking as her beauty.

"Meat," Aiwen said, much to Tanyth's amusement and causing him to chuckle under his breath. "What I meant…" Aiwen kicked his leg under the table. "Was a meat dish, with potatoes, or something? Please."

The waitress flashed a smirk at Tanyth, finally catching on, and nodded her head. "We can do that. And for you?" She turned to Tanyth again.

"I'll have the same," he said. "And we'll both have water."

"Perfect, I'll bring it right away." With that, she strode away through a door that lead to the kitchen.

"You're a child," Aiwen scoffed.

"I've been told…. multiple times."

"We must set off again after we've eaten. I've already packed both of our bags, and they're ready to go in our rooms when we are."

Tanyth nodded. "It seems like a pleasant village."

"It reminds me too much of Elorin."

"I'm glad you thought so too," Tanyth said. "I can't lie. The similarities are rather remarkable."

"I'm definitely the most homesick I've ever been this entire *adventure*."

The boys laughed anxiously together, glad they were both struggling and not alone with their feelings. Silence fell over their conversation until Tanyth finally spoke.

"Do you think she's ok?"

"We've gone over this," Aiwen said sternly, clearly not wanting to overthink the situation. "She is probably on her way to Aralva as we speak."

"Right, but what if she isn't?"

"She is."

"But—"

"She *has* to be," Aiwen snapped. He slumped his body forward over the table and let his eyes shut. This was precisely what he didn't want. "I'm sorry," he said as he raised his head.

Tanyth reached for his hand under the table and gripped it hard.

"You're right," Tanyth said. "She's on her way to Aralva, and we'll be too soon."

AT THAT MOMENT, THE WAITRESS REAPPEARED WITH two glasses of water. She placed them down and walked away but stopped herself in her tracks a few lengths away. She spun her head toward the boys, who were now looking directly at her. "I'm sorry for intruding, but before, were you talking about Aralva?" She said, her voice still sweet and innocent.

Aiwen looked to Tanyth and back to her. "Who is asking?"

The woman's mouth formed an O shape. "My apologies, my name is Imra." She unexpectedly took a seat beside Tanyth. It showed a brave woman to trust two men so quickly. Tanyth admired that. "I couldn't help but overhear your travels to Aralva."

Aiwen shifted uncomfortably in his seat, bewildered by what to say. He couldn't confirm her statements, but she already heard them. He wanted to kick himself for not being quieter.

Imra noticed his plight and leaned closer. "It's ok. I have been to Aralva before."

"You have?" Aiwen couldn't hide his surprise.

She nodded her head. "Yes, I was born there but moved away when I was young."

Tanyth let out a mighty laugh. The relief practically oozed from his frame. "You don't know how good it feels to speak to someone about this."

Imra smiled. "You're travelling there for the first time?"

"We are," Aiwen said, still hesitant about giving too much away.

"I hope I don't sound too forward, but may I join you?"

Tanyth shrugged his shoulders. "I don't see why not."

"May we ask why?" Aiwen said quickly. His gaze shot to Tanyth, his eyes furious. How could they trust someone so quickly? It was all very convenient.

Suddenly, Imra's demeanour changed greatly, and her once bubbly personality disappeared. "You'll think I'm crazy, but these past few weeks, I've felt something off." She swept the hair that fell in front of her eye line from her face. "I think there's something wrong in Aralva… It's most likely nothing, but I've never had this feeling before. Like something is brewing. I just thought it better to be safe than sorry."

Aiwen and Tanyth looked at each other, knowing in their eyes. Imra and Aralva must have a connection, somehow. However, Aralva was extraordinary, so it didn't rattle them too much.

"Imra, that is why we're going to Aralva," Tanyth said whilst eyeing Aiwen, making sure he wasn't over sharing. He inclined his head toward hers. "Naesaela has awoken."

Aiwen crumpled his face and buried it in his palm. He knew they were being too trusting, but what did they really have to lose?

A gasp escaped her mouth, causing the surrounding people to crane their necks. Imra nodded them away, to which they obliged, and turned back to the boys. It seemed she had some authority around her. That or they genuinely respected her and wanted to ensure she was ok. "Are you sure?"

Aiwen grabbed the hem of his shirt and raised it to show his still bloody laceration. "Very sure."

Aiwen and Tanyth told Imra everything for the next ten minutes, only stopping when she left to collect their food. Aiwen had given in to his doubts and told her anyway. What was the worst that could happen?

"So you grew up with Alleria?"

"How did you know her name?" Aiwen asked, his brows arching. He was sure he hadn't mentioned her by name.

"Born in Aralva, remember?" Imra laughed. "We would have daily updates on whether she had been found. It was a whole ordeal."

"Oh," Aiwen said. He was still nervous, and a basic explanation like that had slipped his mind. Of course, she would have known her name. She was the most important prophecy in Aralven history, after all. "Well, yes. All three of us have grown up together."

"Well, unlike the council, I'm pleased she got to experience a normal life and be with family."

Tanyth smiled. "What about your family?"

"My father died when I was little, and my mother lives in Innai. It's a small—"

"You're joking," Tanyth said, holding back a laugh. "That is where Alleria was headed to before Aralva."

"So, the plan is to go there first?"

"It was," Aiwen said. "But that was days ago now. I assume it is perhaps best to make our way straight there."

"Sounds like a decent plan. When do you wish to leave?"

"As soon as possible."

"Alright, I'll meet you outside the inn in twenty minutes," Imra said, already on her feet. She picked up the now empty plates and glasses and began to stride away. "Oh, as well." She craned her neck. "Don't forget to pay Jessamine. Otherwise, she'll hunt *you* down." She giggled to herself before disappearing through the kitchen door once again. Surely she was joking, but then again, Jessamine was a scary figure.

"THAT WENT WELL," TANYTH SAID, STANDING UP himself. He brushed the crumbs from his tunic and stretched his arms.

"Do you trust her?" Aiwen said sharply, still uncertain. In less than an hour, they met her, explained their plans, and agreed to travel with her. It was a lot at once, but their life certainly was crazy. They hoped to the Light she had good intentions.

"Having an Aralvan local with us? That could make our travel time so much quicker."

Aiwen stared at nothing, pondering. "I think you're right."

"I always am."

"That is very debatable."

"Anyway, we still have our weapons if anything goes south."

Aiwen nodded his head in agreement and rose to his feet. He dropped a few coins on the table and strode toward the door they entered through. Jessamine sat unmoved from her seat, glaring as the boys entered the room.

"Does she always have to stare like that?" Tanyth said into Aiwen's ear.

As they reached her desk, Aiwen pulled out more coins from his pocket and handed them to the woman. She inclined her head in her way of thanks.

Moments later, they were back in their room, grabbing their bags, ready to find Aralva.

CHAPTER 21

They kept their heads low.

Alleria's boots clicked on the stone road.

Faces turned to them.

Whispers.

ALNOR THREADED HIS ARM THROUGH ALLERIA'S and picked up the pace until they were at a light jog.

"Yes, because this doesn't look conspicuous at all," Alleria whispered. Though her head was down, she still took in the surrounding sights. For the first time, she saw the open markets and bustling crowds, not all lined with human frames. Species she didn't even recognise clouded her view, a true sight to behold. To avoid seeming rude, her gaze danced away to the clock tower, the one from her dreams and nightmares. But unlike her dreams, it displayed a time.

They'd almost made it through the first street when a young woman cried out Alnor's name. Despite so much time passing, he clearly hadn't changed much. He muttered something under his breath and ignored her yells. He hastened his step, and in turn, Alleria did too.

"Alnor, is that you?" she yelled again.

He didn't hide his frustration, yet behind that lay longing. He wanted to stop and catch up, but he couldn't. They couldn't. Alleria watched the inner turmoil spiral in his eyes; she didn't know what to say. Reluctantly, Alnor threw the woman a smile and a cursory hello, then rushed Alleria into an empty side street. He bent his knees and rested his hands upon them, sharp breaths escaping his mouth. Alleria opened hers to speak, but Alnor raised his hand.

She leaned against the wall, exhausted. They'd only been walking for five minutes, but they were still worn out from the journey here. Alleria guessed his need for rest was more than just for physical reasons. Then she sank to the floor, not caring if her clothes got ripped from scraping them on the wall. She had much bigger problems to worry about. Clothes were the least of her worries. Besides, they were in the all-knowing and magical Aralva. She was sure they would have a spare change of clothes.

"She was a childhood friend," Alnor said. "As much as I want to go and speak with her, we need to find the council right away. I'm an awful liar and the fewer people know about Naesaela, the better."

A chuckle escaped Alleria. "Don't you think," Alleria stopped for a moment, thinking about the best way to phrase what she wanted to say. "Don't you think the people have a right to know what is going to happen?"

"Yes," Alnor said without a second thought. He was standing straight, his voice as sure as she'd ever heard it. "But unfortunately, I'm not in the council's good books, and I don't want to upset them even more."

"That's understandable. But you must remember, as long as you're with me, you're under my protection."

"I'd like to think so, but the council… are dubious. They lie, deceive, twist your words."

"You think they'd go against me?"

"Not necessarily. I think they'll promise you

certain things and take them away once they've gotten *their* way. They've always been like that."

"Sounds like most leaders in Malmar," Alleria said.

Alnor smirked. "Don't let them hear you say that."

"It's not like they can kill me," Alleria said, shrugging, a smile creeping onto her face.

Alnor stretched out his hand to lift her up. "Don't test them," he said whilst hauling her to her feet.

"Where to now?" Alleria's eyes darted to the side street entrance, where they entered, and further down the alley. Luckily, no one had followed them, not even Alnor's friend. Strange.

"If we follow this alley," He pointed down the dark side street. Despite it being daytime, the houses arched over the street, blocking out any sunlight. They could only see so far down until it faded into darkness. It reminded Alleria of the forest. She shuddered at the thought. Too many terrible memories were connected to that forest. "It will eventually lead us to the town hall. The council should be there since it's still daytime."

Alleria nodded. "Are you nervous?"

"To stand in front of the group of people who killed one of my closest friends and have the power to do the same to me?" Alnor pulled at his sleeves and tucked in his shirt before looking to Alleria. "No, not at all."

Alleria laughed. She admired his courage and, at that moment, realised Alnor was the closest thing she ever had to a father. Despite only knowing him for a handful of days, they had grown relatively close. They shared stories of her mother, and Alnor had told Alleria stories of her father. She'd learned more about him in these past two days than her mother in twenty years. He seemed like a great man, but she couldn't help but feel disconnected from him. For that, Alleria would be wary of the council. They already murdered her father and, second-handedly, her mother. She would not let them manipulate her, and she would save Malmar on her *own* terms.

THE PAIR MADE THEIR WAY THROUGH THE STREET, utter darkness shrouding their vision.

"I don't suppose you could light it up a little?" Alnor suggested.

Alleria's mouth gaped, unbeknownst to Alnor. She was still hesitant about using her powers, especially so close to hundreds of innocent people.

After a moment of silence, Alnor seemed to acknowledge Alleria's uncertainty.

"It's alright—"

"No, I'll try," Alleria interrupted. She had to stop fearing who she was... what she was. "I'll try," she repeated. She stopped in her tracks and closed her eyes. It felt strange to do since it was so dark, but she did it anyway.

"Take your time," Alnor reminded her.

She raised her hands from her side and rubbed them together in preparation. Taking a deep breath, her mind ran wild. She thought about her mother and her friends. Emotion was the key to getting her magic to work, much to her dismay. Her chest throbbed at the thought of her mother's lifeless body, but then, she felt a warmth in her palm. She cupped her hands together, curving them into a ball. She didn't let her thoughts falter. Pyria. Aiwen. Tanyth. Father. The heat between her palms was pleasant. She drew her hands away from each other, the ball shape formed. She felt the heat grow as she did so.

"Alleria," Alnor's deep voice cut through her silent concentration.

AT THAT, SHE OPENED HER EYES. HIS FACE FULLY lit, as were her surroundings. Everything was cast in a tender golden hue. It was beautiful. As daunting as using her power was, it was a sure sight to behold. Finally, she lowered her gaze to her hands. A brilliant ball of light hovered between her palms, causing her eyes to squint. However, she couldn't stop looking. She was stunned by the beauty and power inside her.

"It doesn't get old, does it?" Alnor said.

"No, it doesn't," Alleria said with a stifled laugh. She opened her hands, freeing the ball of the golden sun from her grasp. She didn't expect it to work, but she marvelled as it floated forward, seemingly guiding them down the side street. Magic. Real magic.

"Now, that is incredible."

Alleria thought the same. "Well, this is very convenient."

She could see the end of the street now. They weren't too far away, but the light was unquestionably an excellent test of her powers. She didn't *need* to be in danger or use it offensively. She could use this to her advantage, even prove to the council her power should they prove skeptical.

THEY TOOK NO TIME IN WAITING AROUND. MINUTES later, they were standing in front of the town hall. The street surrounding was not nearly as busy as the main square. Fewer people turned to them, and Alleria didn't catch anyone whispering about them. Alnor placed his hand on the door handle, and before opening, turned to Alleria.

"Are you sure?" He asked, the sincerity and worry of a father percolating in his tone. He released his grasp from the handle, awaiting her response.

"Yes," Alleria responded soon after. She had waited so long to get here. She didn't want to waste another minute more.

"Very well." Alnor gripped the handle once again and pushed the door open.

THE ROOM WAS EMPTY, EXCEPT FOR A LARGE TABLE of people at the very top of the room. Lit candelabras decorated the walls, wax dripping onto the floor below. They didn't care too much about the mess. Other than the spilt wax, the room was immaculate. No dust could be seen on any surface, and brass doorknobs were polished to perfection. As they made their way through the long room, the heads of what Alleria assumed to be the council did not raise. They stayed focused in conversation as if Alleria and Alnor didn't exist. Paintings of people Alleria didn't recognise littered every bit of free wall space. She did not expect to recognise them.

Noticing her glances, Alnor leaned in close to her until his mouth was inches from her ear. "The paintings are of the council of past and present."

"I see," Alleria responded, annoyed she hadn't put two and two together. Thoughts of her mother still muddled her mind, so much so, she hadn't put something so obvious together. "They're very… off putting."

The group of people still sat unmoved by Alleria's presence. Surely, they'd be ecstatic for the saviour's return.

"They have always been a fan of theatrics."

"Do you think we should have gone to Ayen first?"

Alnor shook his head. "Ayen is a direct contact with the council. They won't be far away anyway—"

"Speak your name and business," an elderly man interrupted without raising his face from the paperwork in front of him. He looked human, but Alleria knew anything was possible in Aralva. She expected him to stand from his seat and have hooves for all she knew.

Alnor coughed, clearing his throat. "Alnor Sylren."

The man raised his brow, but not his gaze.

Alnor looked to Alleria for her to state her name.

"Alleria Valrona."

AT ONCE, THE SEVEN MEMBERS OF THE COUNCIL raised their heads in unison. Some looked stunned; others' emotions didn't change. The man who had spoken first pushed back his chair and paced swiftly to Alleria.

"Alleria Valrona in the flesh," he said as he strode to her. Much to Alleria's dismay, he had human feet. She found it weird the council was all human in a village of so many mythical and marvellous creatures. "We have been awaiting your arrival for a very long time. And you, Alnor. It has been a great while since we've seen your face around here."

Alnor shot him a fraudulent smile. "I think that is obvious as to why."

The man inclined his head and muttered something under his breath.

"I am aware of Naesaela's growing power. I've even experienced it firsthand," Alleria said before he could say anything further.

The man's face surprised her, confusion spreading in his features.

"We are aware of the evil's increasing power, but, in fear of revolts, we have informed no one.

How have you come to know of this information?"

"I have had dreams and spoken to Ayen Morgwyn through them."

"Have you now..." The man craned his neck to the other council members, as if he were asking if they knew Ayen had been in contact. The shock on their faces mirrored his own. "Ayen had not informed us of their contact with you. When did you speak last?"

"Almost a week ago."

"Interesting. I assume your powers have manifested by now?"

"Yes, they have." Without a query, Alleria raised her hand. This time, she didn't feel the need to close her eyes for a display so small. She felt the warmth grow inside her and trickle down her arm before a small light appeared in her palm. She held it for a moment and then scrunched it between her hands, putting the light out.

A SLOW CLAP ERUPTED FROM THE COUNCIL MEMBERS.

"Incredible," the man croaked. "It seems you have control over your power already. However, it is not enough; you will be put into training right away."

"Right now? But—"

"Evil does not wait, Alleria. We must start now."

"May I know your name before I'm taken away?"

The man chuckled to himself. "My name is Ruven Carqen."

"What about the rest of you?" Alleria motioned to the rest of the council members.

"There will be other times for you to learn their names. For now, you train."

"I just would like—"

"You are here to train!" Ruven's voice pounded in her head. He hadn't shouted, but it reverberated the walls as if he did.

Alleria slowly nodded.

"Now, will we be expecting any more of you? Your mother?"

Alleria did not answer. Instead, her head fell low, instantly, her eyes becoming glassy.

Ruven understood right away. "I'm sorry for your loss. She was an exceptional woman."

Her head shot up. "Yet, you drove her away? And killed my father."

"There are consequences in Aralva."

"I was a child." Her voice was at a shout now, and tears rolled down her face.

"A child with a prophecy."

. . .

ALLERIA STEPPED FORWARD, BUT ALNOR HELD HER back, his arm in front of her.

"Don't," he whispered to her.

Alleria stepped back to where she stood before. The council eyed her from where they sat, enthralled in the conversation.

"I have two friends who should arrive in Aralva soon," Alleria said sternly. She wanted to unleash her power and destroy Ruven for what he did to her family. But she knew that would get her nowhere. They needed as many people as possible to kill Naesaela. She needed the council around... for now.

"Very well," Ruven said. "You will be taken to train right away." He looked Alleria up and down. "And to retrieve some new clothing."

Alleria glared at him. She knew he was right, but she hated he had something to say. It seemed Ruven would do anything to get her riled up.

"It will be fine," Alnor said. "I'll stay with you—"

"No, you will not."

"Ruven—"

"Alnor Sylren, twenty years ago, you escaped Aralva and took the menagerie with you. Did you really assume it would go unpunished?"

"The creatures are healthy."

"You overlook the point. You broke the law, and you will be tried."

Alleria stepped forward once again. "No, he will not." Her voice defiant.

"Alleria, stay out of this," Alnor said.

Alleria ignored Alnor's pleas. For once, *she* would save *him*. "If you want to keep your tongue, you will let him go free."

"You wouldn't dare," Ruven said. "You are merely a child."

"A child of prophecy." Then, without a word, Alleria shot a bolt of light to the painting above the council members. The painting burned for a moment before going out, charred and unrecognisable. She almost laughed at Ruven's jump in fear. The council couldn't hide their terorr… as much as they tried to.

"Next time, it'll be more than a painting."

RUVEN LOOKED TO THE REST OF THE COUNCIL AND then to Alleria. "You do not want to do this, Alleria. Do not make us the enemy."

Alleria scoffed. "You made yourselves the enemy the moment you murdered my father… But… I am willing to put that aside to save Malmar."

"Do you really think Pyria would want—"

Alleria shot her hands up, lighting blaring out. Anger. The bolts beamed upward, carving perfect holes in the ceiling. The council members screamed, yet Ruven didn't.

"Never speak her name again," Alleria yelled. She closed her fists and lowered her arms. "Alnor comes with me."

"Very well," Ruven said reluctantly. He lost his assertive and dominant tone. *Pathetic.*

Alnor grazed Alleria's arm, motioning her to stand back. When she did so, he whispered to her. "Do not let the darkness overcome you, Alleria. It is not worth it."

A few moments later, a timid young boy entered the room, visibly nervous. He was dressed well, and it wasn't until he closed in did she realise he wasn't human at all. Two further legs trailed behind the first two… a centaur.

"Alleria, and Alnor, you will go with Petré to the training grounds." Ruven's voice was shaky. He hadn't expected Alleria's sudden outburst. Neither had Alleria. "You will train through nightfall, for we fear Naesaela will break free any day now… I hope for all of our sakes, we fear wrong."

CHAPTER 22

"Where is she?" Aiwen said, his head peeking around the wall of the inn. "It's been thirty minutes already!"

Tanyth rolled his eyes and pulled Aiwen away from where he dawdled. "Ai, we're not supposed to be drawing unwanted attention to ourselves. And you are very much doing that." Tanyth eyed the passersby, who were gawking at them. "See?"

Without glancing to check, Aiwen nodded. He was always paranoid about one thing or another, but he was sure Tanyth understood. Everyone had their quirks. Tanyth brought his hand to Aiwen's face and lightly slapped it. He giggled as Aiwen's face jolted in shock, thinking it was a loving moment.

"I've got to keep you on your toes," Tanyth

said, a chuckle brewing in the rear of his throat. The boys stumbled over each other, not realising someone standing beside them until their voice penetrated their loving silence.

"OH GOSH, ARE YOU TWO..." IMRA WINKED. *"Together?"*

Imra stood, hands on her hips, with a jubilant expression on her face. She changed into an all-brown outfit accompanied by a large matching bag she lugged over her shoulder. She was definitely dressed for the occasion.

Tanyth nodded while Aiwen shook his head, causing Imra to tilt her neck in confusion.

"I think you two need to decide whether or not you are." She squinted her eyes, thinking. "Did that make sense? I just said a bunch of very similar words, and I—"

"We're together," Tanyth interrupted, putting his arm around Aiwen. "We just weren't sure how acceptable it is around here."

The realisation struck in Imra's eyes. She nodded in understanding. "Oh, I see!" She squealed. "And oh no, you have nothing to fear about that in Taerel. I myself am privy to other women, you see..."

Imra's voice trailed out, and only one word lingered in the boy's minds.

TAEREL.

THEY HADN'T EVEN THOUGHT TO ASK WHAT THE village was called. They'd been so worn out; it hadn't even crossed their mind.

"Well, that's good to know," Aiwen said. Still, he stepped away from Tanyth, not fully trusting Imra's words. Still paranoid.

Tanyth didn't withhold his pained glare, but Aiwen didn't notice. He wished Aiwen would stop pulling away all the time. It worried him. He did whatever he could to make him comfortable, but it still wasn't enough. Wanting to change the subject, Tanyth motioned to the grassy horizon that was somewhat visible behind the village walls. "Are we going that way?"

"There about," she said, looking off into the distance. "So we're definitely skipping Innai and travelling straight to Aralva?"

Aiwen looked to Tanyth to check. He nodded warily. "Yes."

"Great, we will travel northeast then."

"Are we leaving now?"

"Yes, right now."

NO ONE PAID THEM ANY REGARD AS THEY TRUDGED through the bustling streets of Taerel. They assumed that being with Imra diverted any suspicion people would have for newcomers. Taerel didn't seem like the place to have a lot of visitors anyway, so Imra was definitely a big help. They hadn't heard of the village before, and didn't recall it on the map in the book from the library. Taerel must have gone by a different name when the map was drawn, or it might not have existed at all back then. It was a mystery, but it didn't matter. None of this would if Alleria didn't reach Aralva.

As little as they spoke about it, all Aiwen could think about was her. He presumed Tanyth was the same. They had both been superstitious about speaking things into existence, so they tried not to mention if she was alive. However, internally, Aiwen was sure it was the only thing both of them could think about.

They rounded a corner, revealing a way out of the village. It was not the same gate they entered through, but it looked similar enough. The gates were open and bolted to the floor. Aiwen wondered if they ever locked them shut because they were open in the middle of the night before.

A few steps later, they were out of the village. Imra breathed in the warm air as if she had stepped into a new world and was going outside for the first time. The boys didn't query it, for she seemed like quite an unconventional person, anyway. Then again, she was Aralvan; they saw the world differently from the rest of Malmar. The boys knew the existence of such things where the impossible seemed… possible.

"ISN'T IT JUST BEAUTIFUL?" IMRA SPOKE. SHE stopped walking in awe at the emerald landscape. "It reminds me of Aralva… all the green."

"It does look quite similar," Aiwen confirmed.

"You have seen a painting, I assume?"

Aiwen stuttered in his words. "I've seen it in Alleria's dreams. It's…." He struggled to put it into words. "It's hard to explain, but I've seen it."

"You two really have been through a lot, haven't you?"

Tanyth nodded. "That is an understatement."

Imra cast a forced smile, laced with empathy. "You both have done amazing to get this far. I'm sure it's been challenging."

"Thank you," Aiwen murmured.

"I assume you don't travel a lot either?"

"No, not at all."

"I understand how that can be a shock to the system then," Imra said. She brushed her hands through her onyx hair. Somehow, her hair fell back into place like she had never touched it. *Maybe perfect hair was her magical power,* Aiwen thought to himself.

"I travel to and from Aralva from time to time, just to see old friends. However, I haven't heard from my mother in quite a while since she insists on staying in Innai."

"Why's that?"

"My uncle." She rolled her eyes. "No, I don't mean that. The eye-roll, I mean. Basically, he left Aralva twenty years ago because they executed his friend. My mother went with him in protest and just never returned."

Tanyth quirked his eyebrow. "You say his friend was killed?"

"Yes, the saviours—" Realisation struck in her eyes. "By the Light, was that Alleria's father?"

"I believe so."

"Wow, it has been so long since my mother recounted the story, I just never put two and two together. But then again, my uncle always left parts out of the story." Imra walked again, not checking to see if the boys were ready or not. She seemed instinctive like that. It was clear she wasn't used to having company, so they didn't question it.

"So, your mother and uncle are in Innai right now?"

"Yes."

Tanyth's eyes swelled, remembering what Pyria had said to Alleria before she was killed. "That is why Alleria had to get to Innai." He expressed to Aiwen, who, by the look on his face, just caught on. "Pyria knew they would be there to help Alleria."

"Oh, Light," Aiwen said, his voice suddenly less sombre, his posture ringed less from paranoia. The boys beamed.

"I don't mean to bring down the mood," Imra said. "But that is if Alleria made it to Innai. From what you told me, you don't even know if Alleria survived the wolf attack."

SUDDENLY, AIWEN RETURNED TO HIS OLD LETHARGIC self, the reality of the situation invading his senses again. The world seemed to shrivel around them; their stupidity and hopefulness were laid before them, mocking them. Tanyth saw Aiwen's heart break. He didn't need this.

"That is true, but there is no harm in hope," Tanyth said. Despite his own sadness, he built a wall, and overcame it, so Aiwen could feel better. "When my mother passed, I worked through all her journals."

Aiwen raised his head.

"Each day, my mother would journal. Every night, after she put me to bed, she'd stay up writing about how her day went. And she would always write a quote. There were so many beautiful ones, but one always stuck with me. It was written on the day of my father's passing... 'Hope is the one thing that can help us get through the darkest of times.'"

Aiwen reached for Tanyth's hand and squeezed it tight. For once, Aiwen displayed his affection, and not the other way around. Tanyth looked at him, a smile appearing on his lips. They had their relationship scuffles, but they always seemed to work it out. Relationships were never easy, and they had to make sacrifices to keep them healthy.

"That is rather beautiful... and absolutely true," Imra said, drying her eyes. "I'm sorry, I cry at almost everything." The boys chuckled, to which Imra joined soon after. She had brightened the mood for the better.

• • •

"I THINK ALLERIA IS GOING TO LIKE YOU," TANYTH claimed.

"You think?" She replied excitedly. They were confused at her excitement at first but then remembered how Alleria was a literal prophet. Imra had grown up learning about and worshiping Alleria. She was like a queen to her. It was strange—Alleria was just a normal girl.

"Of course," Aiwen said. His gaze strayed to the extensive land ahead and the journey that awaited them. Despite the treacherous trips, he was glad for the company, only wishing Alleria was with them too.

Imra picked up her pace, a newly found skip in her step. She had done wonders for the morale of the group. Tanyth wasn't lying before. Alleria really would like her.

"It is a simple journey from here," she added. "We could be there by tomorrow morn."

"Could?" Tanyth asked.

"Depends on how fast we walk. As you can perhaps surmise, I'm not used to having company on journeys like this."

Immediately, the boys sped up their walk. It wouldn't last long, but for that moment, they were determined. They were just out of Alleria's grasp, and they would not waste another waking moment apart.

"I was thinking," Tanyth said. "Why *has* Naesaela suddenly gone quiet?"

"How do you mean?" Imra asked.

"Before, she was possessing creatures and even the people of Elorin to kill Alleria. Then she glamoured our surroundings to send us off her trail. But since? Nothing."

Aiwen did not have an answer.

Imra opened her mouth to speak before closing it again. Tanyth noticed.

"What is it?" He asked, concern burrowed beneath his soft features.

"It's just…" Her voice quivered. "If Naesaela was about to break free, she would need all of her power fixated in one location."

"The mountain."

"Indeed."

Tanyth stopped walking. "So it will be sooner than we think." It wasn't a question. It was a fact.

"I fear that's true."

"Then, let us not squander for another moment."

CHAPTER 23

The training ground wasn't what Alleria expected at all.

When they curved the corner, a considerable outdoor training facility overcame her view, Alleria did not bury her wonder. The young centaur who guided them surrendered a bow and trotted off. Alleria presumed he was returning to the council, to which she felt for him. But as far as she knew, he could be even older than her. She didn't know how centaurs aged, and at what rate. Having these queries still made her chuckle. A part of her hadn't accepted that this was her life now. She was in the place from her childhood stories… that was sure to take some to getting used to.

. . .

SHE LET HER EYES GLAZE OVER HER ENVIRONMENT. She presumed nearly two hundred humans and even more creatures trained in front of her. However, her eyes instantly concentrated on the arrows firing to her right. She expected a singular room with a multitude of weapons, but this was something else. A small tent was set up beside a small river, people fired across the water. It was not too different from the set-up she trained at in Innai with Alnor.

"It's marvellous, isn't it?" Alnor croaked, emotion flooding through his voice. Had it not hit him fully that he was back in Aralva? He threw a glance to Alleria. "I just want to say thank you for what you did in there. You did not have to do that."

"I did have to do that, Alnor," Alleria argued. "You have been loyal to my mother and father for twenty years. Now, I am loyal to you."

"But Alleria—"

"No buts, Alnor. Friends stick up for each other."

To that, a joyous smile lurked on his face. "Friends," he echoed. "I have not had one of those since your mother."

"Well, get used to it!" She cast him a sarcastic wink and shuffled forward. "Where to first?"

Alnor walked beside her. He was already a

father figure for her and it had only been a few days. "I would have thought they'd have someone to train you personally," he said, peering around, looking for someone, anyone. "But I don't see—"

"ALLERIA VALRONA," A FOREIGN VOICE STATED behind them.

Alleria jerked her body around, as did Alnor, to find a short, stubby man. His hair greyed and face full of wrinkles more than Alleria had seen in her life. Looking to have lived through many a lifetime, she instantly realised he would be the one to train her.

"That am I," Alleria said. She didn't know what she was up for, or even if she had enough time *to* prepare. But she'd try.

"I see your parents in you," the short man said. Seemingly ancient blue robes cascaded across his body. Alleria couldn't deny their beauty and craftsmanship. They were mesmerising. Material like that was unheard of in Elorin. The man studied Alnor, letting his eyes drift up and down his body. "Alnor," he said, a tone in his voice Alleria couldn't place.

"Gaelin Errieth," Alnor said. "It has been a long time."

"Too long," Gaelin corrected. "I must say, I'm astounded you are not in an Aralvan dungeon right now."

"We have Alleria to thank for that."

"Ah, using your importance wisely, I see." The old man forced a laugh. That is when Alleria noticed the sizeable wooden staff in his right hand. It was almost the same length as his body. The tip of it encrusted with a red gem. *A ruby,* Alleria assumed.

ALNOR CAUGHT ALLERIA'S STARES. "GAELIN IS Aralva's finest sorcerer."

Gaelin nodded his head.

"And oldest," Alnor said, to which Alleria laughed.

"Enough of that," He raised his hands, his staff not leaving his grasp. "I may be the finest, but I am unable to fight anymore. My age hinders my dispensation of power... Anyway, we must get to training right away. Will you be joining us, Alnor?"

"It seems so."

"Very well," Gaelin point his finger at him. "Just do not get in my way."

Gaelin strode forward and into the multitude of training sessions; Alleria and Alnor followed.

They managed to evade the swings of swords and axes before ultimately reaching an empty tent. Under it, a table sat, untouched.

Placing his staff down, Gaelin took a seat in the chair stationed behind it. "Show me a glimpse of your power," he said firmly. "I need to see how far along you are."

INSTANTLY, ALLERIA STEPPED FORWARD AND performed the same routine she showed the council. Gaelin smirked as the ball of light appeared in her hands and disappeared as she pleased. She could have never imagined it would come so easily to her.

"Very good."

"She can do a lot more than that," Alnor assured. "You should see the ceiling of the town hall."

Gaelin cocked an eye. "It seems you are very conservative with your power, Alleria. Would that be correct?"

She couldn't help but nod, but it was more out of fear of what she *could* do. She realised she needed to get over herself, but it was easier said than done. Naesaela would not wait for her to get used to her power; she had to quit being a fearful young woman. She was a prophecy. A legend to be feared. Now, she just had to believe it.

"TAKE THIS." GAELIN LURCHED HIS STAFF FROM THE ground and raised it to Alleria's grasp. She took it, confusion lingering on her face.

"Are you sure?"

"Of course," he said. "I would not offer it to you if I was not." He rose from his seat and walked toward her. "This staff was used to seal Naesaela in Mount Tejon. You might need it to destroy Naesaela for good."

Alleria nodded. "You are not afraid to say her name?"

He grinned. "I am not one to believe in superstitions. If…. When Naesaela is free, she will not target just those who spoke her name. It is madness to think like that."

"Finally, someone with sense," Alnor said. "How did you never make the council, Gaelin?"

"I never wanted to be on the council."

"We could do with someone like you representing us."

"There have only even been humans on the council. They would never allow it." He shrugged his shoulders. "Now, stop distracting me." He motioned to an empty spot a few lengths away. "Alleria, stand here, if you will."

SHE OBLIGED, AND AWAITED FURTHER INSTRUCTION, the ancient staff in hand. It rumbled slightly in her grasp, but she tried not to think of it. She knew how powerful it was and she didn't want to use it until she was ready.

"It will not be easy to master the use of the staff. You will need to channel your power from yourself, through the staff, and then out."

"Why use the staff then?" Alleria asked.

"This staff." He placed his hand on the length of the carved wood. "Is made from the ashes of the wood used to burn Naesaela. Dawn wood. The most powerful sorcerers of that time then bound it together. No one knows the logistics entirely, but it seems to be the only thing that can harm her."

"Then why do you require a saviour?"

Gaelin scoffed. "We could probably lock Naesaela in her mountain prison once again, but each time we do so, those bonds become weaker until, eventually." He made a snapping noise with his mouth. "You must destroy Naesaela and set us free from her evil. I am sure you have heard it countless times before, but Malmar needs *you*."

Before Alleria could say anything, Gaelin lightly nudged her forward, commencing their training. He glared at Alnor, a silent command for him to step back out of potential harm's way.

NO ONE HAD GIVEN THEM ANOTHER GLANCE AS they'd sauntered over to their tent—or they hadn't even realised the saviour was back. But they were soon about to learn of Alleria's return.

Gaelin corrected Alleria's posture, forcing her to grip the staff under her left armpit, with her right hand closest to the ruby and her left holding the rest of the weapon. It felt unnatural, like it didn't belong to her. When she expressed her concerns, Gaelin tossed her worries aside. Of course, it didn't feel like hers; she was meant to begin this training twenty years ago. She was two decades behind where the council expected and wanted her to be. Defeating Naesaela was going to be more challenging than she ever imagined. She only hoped she wouldn't crumble under the pressure.

"I want you to feel for your power. Let it brew inside of you," Gaelin said patiently, not wishing to distract her from her concentration.

Alleria did so, and instantaneously she welcomed the warmth of power stirring in her stomach. She nodded. "I feel it."

"Now, when you release the power, imagine feeding it through the staff. Close your eyes. Do not let the world distract you. *Become* your power."

ALLERIA FLUTTERED HER EYES FOR A MOMENT before finally shutting them and the world out. Everything went black. She forced her mind away from the outside sounds and focused on the task at hand. She envisioned the power inside her. It longed to see the light of day, so she let it. In a swift breath, she let the magic free. She felt it travel through her veins and up her forearms, and instead of discharging it straight away, she gripped the staff with more conviction than she had ever before. Her fingers ached at how hard she gripped, but she didn't falter. The warmth trickled through her fingers. She gloried when the staff warmed between her hands.

"MOST EXCELLENT!" GAELIN SHOUTED, BREAKING her from her forced living coma.

She opened her eyes, and all her senses

returned. The sounds of people training around her struck her, and she set her eyes on the staff. It looked the same from the base of it, but as she lifted her gaze, her eyes widened at what she saw. The once red ruby was now adorned in gold. It resounded with power and ached to be released. It longed to be used, to feel actual power.

"Expel the power ahead of you," Gaelin said softly. "Do not be afraid. Trust your power. Trust yourself."

Alleria raised the staff to the position Gaelin had shown her before. Suddenly, it felt right. She felt stronger and more confident in her stance. Digging her heels into the ground, she tightened her grip around the staff. Closing her eyes once again, she took a needed breath. A lot happened at once, but she had never felt so alive. She didn't want this power to fade, because she didn't know life could feel so good.

ON THE EMITTANCE OF HER BREATH, ALLERIA leaned into her stance and pushed the staff forward with all her might. Opening her eyes, she witnessed an arc of sun spew from the tip of the staff. It wasn't a bolt, like in the town hall. The light attracted the glares of everyone around her, though Alleria did not notice nor care. It was controlled like she had been using this power her whole life. She was in her element; she was one with the Light.

A deep crack sounded ....

THUD.

She pulled her weight backwards and lowered the staff. Immediately, the light went out.

What she saw then shook her to her core. The valleys of green that she was enamoured by were gone. Every single hill and tree in front of her before were gone. And she was the culprit. The staff's power.... *Her* power had destroyed such things, and Alleria only felt slightly worn out.

The prophecy was true. She was a deadly instrument crafted by the Light. For the first time, she felt capable and fearless enough to destroy Naesaela. She would need help and a lot more training. But she would do it... she had to.

CLAPS ERUPTED AROUND HER, FORCING ALLERIA TO withdraw into Alnor's presence. She looked at him and noticed he was clapping, too.

"Seriously?" She asked. Her gaze shot to Gaelin, who hadn't moved from where he stood before his mouth gaped.

"Alleria, you are *much* stronger than I thought you to be."

She blushed, not knowing the appropriate response to the statement. She didn't know how to act. The applause still echoed around her, though no one dared to step any closer than the tent. She didn't blame them… she was powerful, but also dangerous and unpredictable. She controlled her power then, but she hadn't in the town hall. Could she even do it again? The human side of her didn't even want to risk it. But the saviour in her knew she had to.

"Alleria, that was quite something," Alnor finally said. He brushed his hand over her shoulder. He hadn't changed or wasn't scared of her. To that, she was thankful. She needed someone to talk to when this was done. Aiwen and Tanyth were still not here, and she only hoped they would show soon.

"IT WAS—"

"Incredible," Alnor finished. He pulled her in for a hug and whispered. "Your mother would be so proud." He released her from the embrace, an authentic smile plastered on his face.

"She kept me away for twenty years. Why would she be proud?"

Alnor sighed. "She kept you away to give *you* a choice. She thought you deserved to have a decision as to whether you wanted to pursue being a warrior of the Light."

"But why didn't she tell me earlier? I only found out because we were attacked."

"I'm sorry, but I can't answer that, for I don't know. But your mother always had a reason for everything she did."

Alleria smiled thinly. "She always did keep secrets, didn't she?"

Alnor chortled. "Your mother was an incredible woman, but oh, did she love to lie."

"Good to know she never changed then, I guess."

Soon, the rampant and somewhat excessive applause died down, and the crowds dispersed, returning to their training. She was glad she was not the only one who would be battling. She didn't work well alone. Family drove her, gave her purpose. That was why Aiwen and Tanyth needed to join her as soon as possible. She could not do this without them. Not anymore.

CHAPTER 24

The sun settled, making it that much harder to navigate their course to Aralva. Luckily, Imra didn't seem to need the daylight to find her way. Despite the darkening skies, she managed to still trek through the endless meadows and forested areas with ease, all while warning them of any sinkholes to avoid. The boys presumed she had travelled to and fro Aralva more times than she had let on.

The boys fell behind, only slightly; mere steps away from Imra, but just enough to have a somewhat unheard conversation.

"I am sorry for all of this," Aiwen spurted out.

When Tanyth looked at his face, he could see something was tearing him up from the inside out.

"For what, Ai?" Confused, Tanyth crested his arm around his loveer's shoulder, where it fit perfectly like they were made *for* each other.

Aiwen sniffled, tears threatening to fall any minute. He brought his hand to where Tanyth's arm rested, just to bask in the familiarity of another's touch. "I'm sorry for the distance, and for pushing you away when I get nervous—"

"Aiw—"

"No, I'm sorry, but let me finish."

Tanyth clamped his mouth shut.

AIWEN CONTINUED, HIS VOICE STILL HUSH, NOT wanting to draw Imra's attention. This was private. "I admit, I am a coward, and I am selfish. I care more about how other people see me than my boyfriend." *Boyfriend.* His voice quirked as he said it; Tanyth didn't show how much it affected him.

"I know it sounds awful," Aiwen resumed, tears beginning to fall. Moisture invaded his sun-dried face. "I do love you. I love you more than anything in this world."

Despite Aiwen's pleas for Tanyth to listen, he spoke anyway. "I feel there is a *but* coming."

Aiwen sniffled again and nodded. His voice grew louder by the word until his cries were at a subdued shout. "But it is out of my control. I cannot help that I feel this way, but it is eating me alive. It invades my dreams, my every waking minute. I cannot do it any longer."

The world seemed to fall silent.

Aiwen was all Tanyth could see, not even noticing Imra stop in her tracks. He knew what was coming before it was even said and felt his heart shatter like it never had before.

"I cannot," Aiwen choked on his words. "I cannot be with you anymore."

TANYTH DID NOT SPEAK. HE JUST WALKED AWAY, A passive fire lighting in his veins. As he passed Imra, she tried to dull the pain, but he ignored her qualms. He blocked out Aiwen's persistent yells for him to return, to listen. But he did not *want* to listen. Not only did he lose his love, but he also lost his friend. A relationship of two decades destroyed by six words. *I cannot be with you anymore.*

The words replayed in Tanyth's mind as if Aiwen was torturously screaming down his ear. The cadence didn't change, nor did the tone. Just a monotonous drone pounding the obvious over and over and over and over.

He knew he was selfish, but he would come to

terms with his own actions later. However, he could not just act like everything was alright, and go back to being merely friends. Aiwen was hurting and was not ready for the relationship. Yet, Tanyth still reacted like he did. He was upset, so he'd act like it. *Anyone going through this situation would react like this,* he kept reminding himself, struggling to justify his action and fight the guilt. He would apologise later, but for now… he needed space, away from Aiwen.

THE TREK WAS SILENT, EXCEPT FOR SOME QUIET whispers between Imra and Aiwen. Tanyth elected not to listen in, worried they were about him. The guilt had devoured him already; he wanted to apologise immediately, but his foolish pride stopped him from doing so. Instead, he floundered on, walking quicker than he had before, until he was at a slow jog. Bounding ahead of the others when something came into view, it wasn't until he was closer, did he realise what it was. It was moving, breathing. A fire.

"Imra?" Tanyth said. His first words in hours were croaky and dry. "Imra." He said again, his voice now as loud as it could go.

Moments later, She was by his side, her face horror-stricken as soon as she saw. It was hard to tell because of the lack of sunlight, but her lip trembled, and she reeled back. She raised her hand to cover her mouth, shocked. "That is not just a fire." she said. "It is a village... It is Kelgeiros."

WITHOUT ANOTHER WORD, IMRA BELTED FORWARD, disappearing into the dark night, a pitch-black abyss, but they didn't worry, for they knew where she was headed. Tanyth looked to Aiwen, glad he couldn't fully make out his expression before running to the burning village himself. The flames were a beautiful nightmare, reds and orange hues burning the night air surrounding it. As they closed in, the heat surged through them both. Even from bounds away, it felt like it could melt their skin. They caught up with Imra, who could not go any further, either. The inferno before them illuminated their view, and Tanyth noticed tears deluging down Imra's face.

"Did you know the village well?" Tanyth asked. His tone was softer than it had ever been, afraid the faintest words could destroy her even more. He knew how it felt to see something you love dearly ripped away.

Imra turned from the fire, unable to watch any further. She raised her head, the light of the blaze backlighting her rather beautifully. "Not extremely well, but well enough. I stop here if I am travelling at night. My friends here have treated me very well over the years, and now… they are gone."

Tanyth stepped forward and offered her his arms, but she declined.

"No, I am ok," she insisted, wiping her nose with the back of her brown sleeves. "I mustn't let this affect me, for that is what Naesaela wants. She wants to slow us down, delay the inevitable. But we must be strong."

"We can rest for a moment," Aiwen spoke. His voice rung clear in Tanyth's mind, and he hated how much it was affecting him. It was just a voice. But it was *his* voice.

"No, we go now." Her tone was harsh and followed by a brisk stomp of her foot. She composed herself and immediately continued on toward Aralva.

CHAPTER 25

"Again."

Alleria huffed, picking up her bow for the thousandth time. Drawing the string, it whistled in the late-night wind, piercing through the empty training ground. Other fighters retired hours ago, but Alleria stayed. As did Alnor. She assumed Gaelin would stay too, but it seemed he trusted Alnor enough to train her himself; he would let her rest when he sought fit.

Alleria released the arrow and power surged through her fingers. Like the last hundred tries, glorious light shot into the arrow before blasting it miles away. It no longer impressed her. She was tired, lowering her bow to her side before abandoning it to the floor in exhaustion.

"What use am I if I am not rested?"

"You're right," Alnor said. He dropped down and retrieved the wooden bow from the ground. Any heat the ground had assimilated from the past sunny day had faded, now ice cold. "We may retire now."

"Thank the Light!" Alleria yelped, already turning to walk back to the village.

"Alleria, wait."

Alleria turned. "Alnor, I am not doing one more—"

"No, it is not that."

Craning her head in wonder, she stepped closer to Alnor.

"I just want to say how well you've done today. I know it has been a lot, and I can only imagine how exhausted you are. Using your power over and over like this is bound to tire you out."

"Thank you," she said. "But could you not have told me that on the way back?" She nudged him playfully and walked away. Alnor rolled his eyes and ran to catch up with her.

"I believe you'll just stay at my house for tonight. Gaelin informed me that no one else has taken residence in it since my departure. Lucky me!"

. . .

ALNOR'S HOME WAS NOT TOO DIFFERENT THAN HERE in Innai. It was slightly more sizeable, but the interior was practically the same. Alleria wondered if it was a common design, or if the design was meant to feel more at home in Innai. Home sickness was a pest.

As they stepped into the living room, a lit fireplace surprisingly greeted them.

Alnor caught Alleria's confused glare. "Fireplaces in Aralva kind of have a mind of their own. They light themselves when the temperature drops to a certain level."

"That is remarkably handy.... and creepy."

"I suppose it is." Alnor laughed. He stepped further into the room and into the conjoining kitchen. The wall had been knocked down to create a large open area. It was cosy. He strode to a metal door, and Alleria hoped mythical creatures wouldn't come flying out. Instead, when Alleria peered over his shoulder, all she saw was food. It was a stocked pantry.

ALNOR TURNED AROUND WITH A MOUNTAIN OF fresh food towering in his arms. "It seems they stocked the pantry for us." Moments later, the food was strewn over the kitchen table as he began to chop vegetables.

"Isn't it a bit late for food?" Alleria asked, not sure if she could even stomach anything. It was partially because of the time of day, but more so, the dread in her veins and the pit at the bottom of her stomach. It was a matter of time before Naesaela broke free, and it didn't feel right to sit around and just eat.

"Yes, it probably is," he said. "But if you have any hope of destroying Naesaela, you will need to get something in you. You need *something* substantial because a weak, malnourished twenty-year-old will not be any match for an ancient evil dragon." He pointed at a wooden stall at the end of the table. "Sit."

HE WAS RIGHT. SHE COULD FEEL HER RIBS THROUGH her tunic, threatening to pierce through her frail skin. They hadn't eaten well this past week, so she needed to make up for her lack of proper nutrition. Her mother adored cooking, and the thought of food always brought her mind back to her.

She took her place at the end of the table, with a newly found hunger as Alnor dropped chopped vegetables into boiling hot water.

. . .

ALLERIA SIPPED THE LAST DROP OF SOUP BEFORE returning the spoon to the bowl.

"It was delicious, Alnor," Alleria said, still licking any remnants from her lips. "My mother never made soup, so this was lovely."

"I will be sure to pass the compliments to my grandmother."

"Your grandmother… is alive?" Alleria did not mean to sound shocked, but she couldn't help it. Alnor was at least fifty years old!

Alnor laughed mightily, hand on chest, his back arched over a chair. "No, she is dead." He grinned again. "But I could be meeting her again soon."

She scoffed. "Well, thank you for the vote of confidence!"

ALLERIA PICKED HERSELF UP FROM THE DINING TABLE chair and walked to the other side of the kitchen. She washed her dish in a bowl of hot soapy water, trying not to flinch as the boiling water spat against her skin. She thought about invoking a barrier of light with her magic, but decided against it. Her powers needed to rest. She wasn't sure if she had the energy to perform such a task, anyway. Her eyes lulled more and more every minute.

"I hope you know I was only joking with you, Alleria," Alnor said, still seated at the table. His eyes looked tired also. They both needed to rest.

"Of course, you have more faith in me than anyone else."

"That is true," he said. "But there is still worry, of course."

"I would be worried if you *weren't* worried."

"Are you scared?" He asked abruptly, his face suddenly stern.

ALLERIA STOPPED SCRUBBING HER BOWL AND TURNED her whole body. "More than I've ever been before. Every time I think about Naesaela, my toes curl and my stomach tightens. I'm always on edge. Then I worry about Aiwen and Tanyth and whether they're alive. For all I know, they're dead in that damned forest. And then, of course, my mother. I'm reminded of her death wherever I turn." Alleria dropped her head.

"Good." That was all Alnor said.

"In what world is that 'good'?"

"It shows morality."

Alleria strode forward and stretched out her hands on the back of the chair beside Alnor. "How is morality going to help me destroy Naesaela?" Not anger, but curiosity.

"Alleria, when will you realise that your morality is your biggest asset. That is the difference between Naesaela and yourself. The love and power of your family, which Naesaela sees as a weakness, drives you. But it's not a weakness. Your power is always at its strongest when defending, or even thinking about your family and friends."

Lips parted, Alleria removed her hands from the chair, pulling it back and took a seat, realisation finally setting in.

"The town hall, that was to protect you." Her voice was soft, calmer than it was before.

"Exactly."

"And when I wiped the evil from everyone in Elorin, that was to save my mother."

"Don't you see?"

"I do," Alleria finally admitted, a shy smile forming upon her lips. It quickly dropped. "But Naesaela is going to be a lot stronger now. She's going to have an army that I'm not going to be able to wipe away instantly."

"That is expected, yes. But we will have an army too."

"Are there plans, and formations, and—"

"Yes," Alnor interrupted. "They have been in place since your birth. There is no need for you to worry about anything else but rest right now.

When Naesaela escapes, we will be prepared. And so will you."

"But what if I can't?"

"Can't what?"

"Can't kill her," Alleria said. All this time, she'd been told she was the saviour. But what if they're wrong? What if she's not strong enough?

"Alleria, you are prophesied—"

"That means nothing. Anyone could have written that. Even if it is true, what if I'm simply not strong enough, or I'm killed before I can kill Naesaela? There are too many variables."

ALNOR NODDED HIS HEAD, UNDERSTANDING HER concern, sharing the same fears by the look in his eyes.

"I think this is exactly what Naesaela wants," he said, raising a hand to her back and patting it tenderly, soothing her brewing tears. "She wants you to doubt yourself, to feel like an imposter. She knows you can destroy her, so she needs to catch you off guard."

Wiping her eyes, Alleria looked up. Alnor gazed lovingly back at her, trying to help. She sighed and leaned into his touch. "It's just so much pressure."

"I know it is. Anyone in your situation would

feel the same." He smiled and pulled his hand back. "Now, let us get you to bed before you fall asleep at this table."

Happy to escape, she laughed. She was glad she had eaten, but she would pay for the lack of sleep in the morning.

ALNOR GUIDED HER TO HER ROOM AND INFORMED her he would wake her when she was needed. She hoped it wouldn't be too early, but she had a feeling it would be. Naesaela didn't seem like one to wait for Alleria to catch up on sleep.

THE ROOM WAS SIMILAR TO THE ONE IN INNAI, almost down to a tee. Alnor really had tried to replicate the home as much as he could. It was admirable, really; it showed how much he really loved Aralva. She traced her fingers on the painted walls. Designs spewed across every side even in lowlight, Alleria could make out the beautiful patterns. Soon, she changed into her nightclothes and escaped into the confines of the freshly made bed, not bothering to draw the curtains unable to cover the beautiful valleys surrounding her. She could watch them for hours. Flashes of a burning Aralva shot into her mind, but she forced it away. She looked to where the mountain layed, suddenly realising she had yet to meet Ayen. They were the reason she was here, and they hadn't even bothered to find her.

Slightly annoyed, she turned her back to the window and finally let her eyes close. Tomorrow would be a new day, in one way or another. She would train and meet Ayen, and hope to the Light Naesaela was not strong enough yet.

CHAPTER 26

Fire and brimstone.

MALMAR WAS NO LONGER MALMAR. IT WAS purgatory. Alleria stood on her bed as the earth melted around her and lava took its place. This was her reality. It was a dream for now, but for how much longer? She didn't dare to step away from her bed, fearing Naesaela was somehow strong enough to harm her through her dreams. No screams left her trembling throat either, for no one would hear and would be a waste of breath. Naesaela taunted her, playing a game. And Alleria was the pawn.

She watched helplessly as the valleys caved in

themselves and magma shot from inside. But Alleria did not cower, nor did she fear what was to come. She was born to destroy Naesaela, and she would do just that or die trying. She placed her hand on her chest, feeling the pool of power inside her. It increased by the second until she couldn't stop it from slipping through her fingers. She let it circulate through her body freely, allaying any manifestation of Naesaela inside her. Suddenly, the charred Aralva landscape faded from view until it was nothing. She was but a girl, glistening like a glorious sun, in a field of darkness.

❄

LOUD KNOCKS FINALLY WOKE ALLERIA FROM HER futile state. Her emerald eyes shot open as Alnor entered the room, his posture radiating nothing but shock. Instantly, she vaulted out of her bed.

"What happened?" She said, suspecting the worst.

Alnor was illuminated by candelabras Alleria definitely hadn't lit herself. It cast his face in a warm golden hue, the tellings of an early morning, but no. As she peered to the window, she realised daylight hadn't broken yet, and it was still dark out.

"Something is entering Aralva's perimeter."

"Aiwen and Tanyth?" Alleria laced her boots and shot to her feet at the words. Her eyes widened, and her lips curved into a hopeful, yet hesitant smile.

Alnor's demeanour did not change. "We are not sure."

"Why are you so apprehensive?"

Alnor motioned to the bed, and Alleria sat next to Alnor. Sweat fell down the nape of her neck, scared of what was about to be said. She gripped her arm for comfort. *Please, be ok,* she thought to herself.

"It very well could be your friends, but...." He paused and bit the inside of his lip. Alleria had grown impatient with Alnor's stunted speech. The anticipation was eating her alive and had enough to worry about, which was not helping.

"But what, Alnor," she said, her voice raised. She didn't apologise when Alnor's face twisted in shock at her tone.

"BECAUSE THEY'VE NEVER BEEN TO ARALVA BEFORE, and they weren't invited in." Alnor twiddled his thumbs. He dreaded what Alleria would say, of what she would do. "There is a defence system around Aralva. It's ancient Elven magic, but we cannot do anything about it."

"Why didn't you tell me?"

"It completely slipped my mind. It is not often a stranger to Aralva enters the perimeter."

Alleria's brows furrowed in confusion. "I am confused. Why are you so worried about it?"

He sighed deeply and dropped his head. "It is likely whoever is in there right now will die."

"No." Suddenly, Alleria let go of his arm, her mouth agape. "I will not allow it," she said, already striding out of the door.

Rosa stood right outside of her room, sadness burrowing in her eyes. She tried to console Alleria, but she would allow nothing to stop her. Her friends were in trouble, and she could not live with herself if she did not try. This wouldn't be the first time she'd disrupted Elven magic. Now, she just hoped she could do it again.

"Alleria!" Alnor shouted. But it was no use. She was gone.

CHAPTER 27

"We're about to enter Aralva's perimeter," Imra said, her eyes on the sandy floor. It seemed she was ensuring she didn't fall into a sinkhole, remarking frequently how they were by where the river splits.

Tanyth raised his hand as if he was a child back in school. "I don't see it?"

She let out a low chuckle. "Aralva is hidden from the eye of wanderers for… many reasons. Even Aralvan natives cannot see past the shroud, they just know where it is. Ancient Elven magic has hidden it for years and will for centuries to come. Right." Imra stopped and swung around to the boys. Her face was blank, but her eyes told a different story. Even the greatest actor struggled to hide their authentic emotion.

• • •

"WHAT IS IT?" AIWEN ASKED. HE IMMEDIATELY noticed the concern hidden behind her eyes.

Before answering, she glanced behind her and then back at them. "This ancient magic is... unpredictable. I don't know how it'll affect you, but just know it will not be pleasant." She sighed. "I cannot help you through, for Aralvans are resistant to the magic, but unfortunately, you... are not."

Tanyth instinctively grasped Aiwen's hand in fear. Moments later, his body caught up with his brain, and he jerked away. "What do you mean?"

"I wish I knew more, but alas."

"So we could die?"

"I'm afraid that is a possibility."

"Well, that would have been good to know before," Tanyth snarled. He ran both of his hands through his wet hair, not being able to tell if it was damp because of the grease from days without bathing, or sweat from the desert heat. He hoped for the latter.

"I didn't want you both to bide in the fear," she said. "It's not a pleasant feeling. The apprehension often hurts the most. But I can tell you...."

Imra's voice trailed off as the boys faced their

fate. As soon as they stepped over the Aralvan boundary, Imra would be gone. They would be alone with only their hope of finding Alleria alive.

MINUTES LATER, IMRA STOOD MOTIONLESS. THE AIR hummed with power and induced them all to shake slightly.

"Can you feel it?" Imra asked.

It was a senseless question. The boys nodded, but it was clear, by their grimaces, that they could. Tanyth clutched his head in hand as he took his place beside Imra. The magic pounded against him, trying to ward him off. It wasn't quite painful, yet it also was.

"I will go first, then you follow after me."

Before they could challenge her, Imra was gone. She had taken just one step and disappeared into, for all they knew, oblivion. There was not a spark or a glow. Nothing. One moment she stood beside them, the next, she was over the invisible border.

Despite his current pained feelings, Tanyth turned to Aiwen.

"Are you ready?" He asked. Moisture beaded on his lip, unsure if it was because of the scorching heat or his nerves.

Aiwen nodded his head. "3."

"2."

"1."

THE BOYS CLOSED THEIR EYES AND STEPPED FORWARD with all their weight. They forced their tired feet through the unseen barrier until the pressure was gone. The incessant hum and pounding in their head had disappeared without a trace. But when they let their eyes flicker open, nothing had changed. They stood in the same small desert, no Aralva insight.

"Where is…"

Tanyth walked forward, already multiple lengths away by the time Aiwen had noticed. "Where are you going?" Aiwen asked.

"Well, we won't get anywhere by just standing here."

"Yes, but we should be careful."

Tanyth didn't turn and only shrugged.

"Tanyth…"

Suddenly, the sand swirled beneath Aiwen's feet wind suddenly picking up. Aiwen didn't stir until he saw the sand before his eyes.

"Tanyth!"

"Aiwen, what!" He shot his body around,

anger creasing his face. But, as he turned, fury dispersed into fear. "Aiwen run, right now."

A FLURRY OF SAND DANCED AROUND TANYTH, hindering his vision. Already, his eyes burnt.

Aiwen took no time in waiting and sprinted forward. His sight was a blur of gold and brown, but he did not stop. Once he reached Tanyth's side, they hurried north, hoping to find the end of the madness. The sand soon encapsulated both of them like a travelling tomb. Every moment that passed, the sand picked up momentum until it was in a full-blown storm.

"Cover your mouth!" Aiwen screamed. The tempest muted his voice, but Tanyth still heard him. They both desperately flung their hands over their mouth, but it was no use. Sand invaded their every sense, sending a roaring pain through them both.

They kept running, hoping their feet didn't fail them. Their eyes burned as the storm lashed at their irises. Unclear where they were running to, they didn't let that fact hinder them. Until Tanyth slowed, and the pain too much for him to bear. He trailed behind, dropping his head low in defeat, but was quickly interrupted by a hand in his. Aiwen pulled him back to his side, not wanting their last time together to be in peril. Despite their differences, he was going to get to Aralva with him or not at all. He'd already made clear he couldn't live a life without Tanyth. Even if they weren't together and didn't speak to one another. He could not live with himself if he was dead, if he could have saved him.

IT WAS TOO MUCH. EVERY STEP WAS HELL. THEY sealed their eyes shut, running frantically through the devilish winds, their hands cupped over their mouths. But little by little, sand slithered through the cracks between their fingers. With every small step, their hands shifted, and sand invaded their insides. Eventually, the boys fell to the floor, plunging their hands downward to catch their fall. Burning from the inside out, Tanyth still pulled himself forward. He grabbed an unconscious Aiwen with his other hand and heaved through the treacherous conditions. He was limp in his grasp, but tears didn't fall. They couldn't fall. His eyes were bone dry, and Tanyth screamed, the last bit of strength yanking Aiwen forward.

Nothing.

He gave up, and didn't bother to clamp his mouth shut as his head hit the floor. They were alone but together. He let his eyes flutter open to see Aiwen for the last time. Through the storm he made out his lifeless body. If he could cry, he would have. Instead, his eyes shut once again.

Suddenly, the winds didn't beat Tanyth's back, the sand slowing down. Then he felt it fall over him. He clawed his way up through the fallen sand that had almost buried him. He coughed as he made it to his feet. But when he finally cleared his eyes of the excess sand and opened them, he stumbled back. It was was all gone, and beyond the tempest lay emerald green. It was a sight he could have only imagined, but he didn't stop in awe. Hurriedly, he dropped to his knees beside Aiwen, shaking his body, hoping death hadn't claimed him yet.

"Come on," he pleaded. "Not again." A tremendous feeling of deja vu flooded his systems. He hated it. It was a rare occurrence to witness your friends die, let alone twice in a matter of a week. Even if they weren't *together*, he needed Aiwen. They had been friends for almost two decades, and Tanyth finally realised that was all that mattered. Not the love. Not the sex—

Just as a tear sparked from his eye, Aiwen shot up.

"What happened? Where's the sand?" His voice was hurried and panicked.

"Hey, hey. You're ok. We made it through," Tanyth said, his tone suddenly bright, yet wobbly and on the verge of tears. He launched his arms around Aiwen, and he let him. They relished in each other's touch, happy they were alive. Happy they were together.

Their bond was soon cut short when harsh yells cut through their *moment*. Their heads twisted behind them, where a blurred figure was running, quite frantically, toward them. Long brown hair floated behind her.

Alleria.

SECONDS LATER, SHE WAS ON THEM, TEARS streaming down her fresh, yet tired, face. She sank into both of their touches and didn't let go. Not this time. Not again.

"I thought you were dead," she said. Her face buried itself in their bodies like she was going to lose them again. When she finally lifted up, the delight on her face was like they'd never seen before. They'd never seen her so happy, so relieved. So content.

"Well, we did too for a good moment," Tanyth joked.

Alleria smiled with her teeth until her face throbbed. Eventually, she clambered to her feet, her hands still grasping for her friend's touch. She missed her mother more than ever. Her dying wish was for them to reach Innai, and she'd done that and more, one step closer to ending this hell once and for all. With Tanyth and Aiwen back at her side, she felt stronger. Like her army suddenly doubled, for family *was* her army.

A sudden presence stepped beside them, causing Alleria's head to shoot in its direction.

"Who is this?"

CHAPTER 28

"I apologise. I truly don't mean to alarm you, Alleria," Imra said. "I came with your friends. But I am a big admirer of you… of your prophecy, not your looks. That's not to say you're not very beautiful, because you are." She squinted her eyes in embarrassment. "Sorry, I will be quiet."

ALLERIA'S EYES DARTED OVER THE WOMAN'S FRAME. She was very beautiful as well. Her coiled black locks slightly unkempt but seemingly not rattled by the storm at all. Her clothes were intact, and her shoes were as worn as the next person's. "Why were you not affected by the storm?" Alleria asked, not trusting her perfect appearance. Being beautiful and having a charming personality did not equate to trust. Although, she could not deny Imra's allure and found her gaze drifting down to her lips. Realising what she was doing, she darted her eyes away.

"She's Aralvan," Aiwen said quickly. At that moment, he got to his feet and smiled his sheepish smile at Imra.

"Good to see you both made it," Imra said. Her nerves were obvious as she rounded one leg behind the other.

"Only just."

"How did you meet?" Alleria asked coyly. She was curious, but her voice rang slightly with jealousy. She wanted to know everything that happened to them, and why it took them so long to reach Aralva.

"Can we do this over some food?" Tanyth butted in, finally getting to his feet. "I am starving."

Alleria chuckled, just relieved they had finally made it. "Of course. I'll take you back to where I'm staying. There is much for you to learn of."

❄

"THANK YOU, AL," TANYTH SAID AS SHE HANDED him some leftover food. She'd just spent thirty minutes heating it over the fire. Alnor's cooking was exquisite, but this looked... interesting. It appeared the food they made the night before didn't reheat very well. Alleria placed a plate in front of Aiwen and made a beeline for her room.

"Now, eat up," Alleria said in a motherly fashion as she stepped through the door. "You're going to need something in you."

Tanyth took a bite and another. His face lit up with every new bite.

With Tanyth's reaction, Aiwen also began eating.

"This is incredible," Aiwen exclaimed, shocked that the food tasted better than it looked.

The door lurched open with a sense of urgency, and Alnor entered. His tired eyes showed no emotion, but he didn't in a rush. "Imra is catching up with some friends and will be right here." He took a seat opposite the boys.

"That's great. Thank you again for making us so welcome." Tanyth said. They'd grown a strong bond with Imra in the past few days, like they'd known each other for years, and the boys didn't want to lose a friend like that. They wanted to stay in touch when they returned to Elorin—*if* they returned to Elorin.

"I hope my niece has treated you well," Alnor said, his focus turned to Aiwen and Tanyth.

"Your niece?" Aiwen asked. Suddenly, it was like a candle was lit in his mind, and everything fell into place. "You're Imra's uncle from Innai. She told us of you but I didn't expect to meet you here as well." He let out a shocked laugh but kept eating his food. Tanyth's reaction was similar, but he seemed too engrossed to show any emotion.

"Yes, I didn't expect to be here either, but it's been a confusing and stressful twenty years," Alnor said. "Imra didn't want to be tied down to Innai, so once she was old enough, her mother let her travel around."

"That must have been hard."

"Family is hard."

"You can say that again," Tanyth said.

"Family is hard."

"No, it was—"

"I'm kidding," Alnor interrupted. He surrendered a mighty howl, which in turn set Alleria off from the other room. "I was not born yesterday. I am up to date with sarcasm."

"Well, now I feel stupid." He laughed.

"However, as I was saying before. Family is hard. We all have to make a sacrifice or two in our lives for our families. That's what my sister, Rosa, did for me." He looked at him and smiled.

She never regretted her decision to leave Aralva for him. "When I left Aralva, so did she. I do not know what the future held, but it is always easier to navigate when you're not alone."

"So I hear," Tanyth said.

"WHERE IS ALLERIA ANYWAY?" ALNOR SAID, changing the conversation. The topic of leaving Aralva seemed to still upset him. However, it was not shocking given his immediate arrest and trial just the day before. If Alleria hadn't stepped in…

"One minute... I'm here." Her voice rang unknown before she stepped through her bedroom door. She changed into her clothes for the day: another pair of brown breeches, and a white shirt. It was what she was comfortable in, and she required a sense of familiarity right now. Sifting through her hair, brushing out any remnants of the night before, she took a seat on an empty armchair. "Last night, I dreamt of Aralva again."

"Like how you did before?" Aiwen asked.

Alleria nodded her head. "It was burnt—it was… hell."

"She's taunting you." Alnor shifted in his seat. "I think she's ready to break free, but she's just waiting for the moment we are least expecting it."

"Wait," Tanyth interjected. "Any time now, she could—"

"Yes, I believe so."

Tanyth rubbed his face in his hands. "Well, that's exciting, isn't it!" His humour was usually well-liked, but his timing was off. No one laughed, and he sunk into his seat, flustered.

"I am almost certain it will be at some point today," Alnor added. "Most likely tonight, when the sun sets. Nighttime gives her an advantage over us."

"Why is that?" Aiwen asked.

"Well, can you see in the dark, Aiwen?" Alnor's tone was harsh, and regret leaked in his face as soon as he said it. "I'm sorry."

Aiwen shrugged.

"Let's get to training then." Alleria rose from her seat before she finished her sentence.

"Wait a moment, Alleria." Alnor raised a hand for her to stop. "Ayen wants to see you."

"It's about time.... Where are they?"

"Townhall."

Alleria twisted her neck and furrowed her brow. "Seriously?" She detested that place—well; she detested the council and aimed to avoid them whenever she could.

"The council is not there this early. You'll be fine."

Alleria's face suddenly composed. "Well, thank the Light for that."

SUDDENLY, THE DOOR CRACKED OPEN AND IMRA appeared on the other side. She changed at some point and now donned a rouge gown that cut off at her ankles, the large rucksack still on her back. "What did I miss?" She called out, closing the door behind her. Even with full hands, she exuded grace.

"Alleria is about to go meet Ayen." Tanyth said distorted, his mouth full of food.

"Well, technically, I've already met them," Alleria corrected.

Imra smiled and hauled her bag through the room and onto a spare chair. "I wish you the best of luck, Alleria Valrona." Despite the sarcasm, a sense of truth oozed from her words.

Alleria crooked her head slightly. "With Ayen, why?"

Raising from her bent over position, Imra dropped her bag and stood straight, her hand on her hips. She glanced to the ceiling, as if she didn't know how to word what she was trying to say. "Ayen is a character, shall we say?"

"What does that mean?" Alleria laughed.

"They can just be quite intimidating, I think." Shrugging, Imra turned back to her bag.

"Right... Well, I love your dress, Imra." Alleria attempted to shift the subject.

Imra quickly spun around. "Goodness, thank you so much! That's the problem working in a brewery... nobody gets the fashion, you know?"

Alleria beamed. "I do, I do. Well, you look beautiful."

"That means a lot coming from such a gorgeous—"

"Alright, alright," Alnor interrupted. "You're going to be late! Alleria, I will be at the training grounds soon, so when you're done, meet me there."

Alleria nodded, said her goodbyes, and seconds later, was on her way to the town hall.

THE STREETS WERE EMPTY, BUT DAWN WAS ONLY JUST breaking. It must have rained in the time they'd been inside because Aralva smelt like petrichor. The smell was so strong, like it was permanently stained into the streets. It was peculiar, but also comforting because of how often rained in Elorin. She missed it so much.

As she continued her course, she smiled at the odd citizen already dressed and out for the day.

They whispered behind her back as she passed by, but she was somewhat used to it by now. They've known about her for decades, so of course, they'd look at her like a spectacle. It just annoyed Alleria that they seemed to know more about her than herself. A whole chunk of her life was hidden from her, and she'd only just cracked the surface of what she was capable of.

Before she could spiral, she looked to the valleys, which instantly took her mind off things. The destroyed ones from the day before were still… destroyed, so she looked to others. Their beauty never neglected to astonish her. The myriad of flowers scattered over them was Alleria's favourite. But it also reminded her of her nightmares, of the chance that all of this could be destroyed. Her stomach flipped at the thought. Her eyeline brushed over the spot where Mount Tejon laid. She made a mental note to ask Ayen to remove the shroud for her. She wanted to see the calm before the storm. She needed to be ready.

THE TOWN HALL LOOKED NO DIFFERENT, EXCEPT FOR the vacant chairs at the end of the room. It suddenly seemed less daunting without the council members there. Their demeanour and presence was … off. As she passed through, the candles came to life, lighting her way. When she reached the empty chairs, she turned around, only to find Ayen standing before her. Alleria tried to hide her intimidation, but ended up stepping back lightly. Their golden hair groomed to perfection, with no stragglers in sight. It was like a sleek wave that never reached the shore. Their face like stonework as if it was refined by the Light itself. Cascades of a red and brown robes fell over Ayen's body so effortlessly. It was stunning.

"ALLERIA VALRONA, YOU CAME." THEIR VOICE WAS silk. And satin. And velvet wrapped into one. It wasn't deep, nor was it high pitched. It was luxurious. Alleria couldn't place it.

"I didn't really have a choice." She smiled.

"There is always a choice," Ayen corrected. "It may not always be obvious, but there is always a choice. You just have to decide whether it is right or wrong."

Alleria wanted to roll her eyes but didn't out of courtesy. Riddles, riddles, riddles. Of course, she didn't have a choice.

"I respect your words, but I didn't have a choice, Ayen."

Ayen's face didn't alter. "Choice is a strange concept, isn't it?"

They made their way to one of the empty seats and took their place. Alleria thought her mind was playing tricks on her, but it seemed as if Ayen glided to the seat. Surely not. She rubbed her eyes and took a seat for herself.

"Now, Alleria… take my hand."

Alleria closed her hand in theirs, and Ayen gripped tight. Instantly, she felt a warmth. It wasn't her power… it felt different. Ayen was searching within her. She didn't know how, but alas. "Alleria, your thoughts are scattered. Try to cleanse your mind, empty your thoughts."

"But—"

"Do it, please."

Alleria gave in and closed her eyes. She wasn't sure how or even if she could stop her wandering mind. Much to her dismay, it did what it wanted to. She tried to force things from inside her, but it didn't seem to work. If anything, she was thinking about them more.

"That is not working, Alleria."

"I don't know how," she said, frustrated.

"Breathe, Alleria. Breathe."

Reluctantly, and with a huff, she loosened up in her seat and took a heavy breath. On the exhale, she imagined her thoughts leaving her mind. She thought of the valleys, their beauty. She thought of the forest, of *its* beauty. Yes, she almost died there, but she couldn't deny how striking the nature was.

SUDDENLY, AYEN JERKED BACK, DROPPING HER hands as they did so. When Alleria opened her eyes, Ayen was gawking back at her with fear dripping from their eyes. It was a terrifying sight to behold.

"This is much worse than I thought it to be."

"What, why?" Alleria's voice raised, and she sat up from her seat. "Ayen, what did you see?"

For the first time, Alleria witnessed Ayen stutter. They were no longer the calm and wise elf she'd known them to be. Instead, their body trembled, and their voice quivered as they spoke.

"I saw death and destruction. It won't just be Aralva or Malmar.... It will be the entire world." Ayen swallowed a knot in their throat. "Alleria, if you do not defeat Naesaela, we will all perish. The extinction is coming."

CHAPTER 29

Alleria joined Alnor at the training grounds, where he tested Aiwen's archery skills. When she appeared beside him, he craned his neck.

"Ah, Alleria, you made it." Instantly, he could feel something off. She looked the same, but her demeanour was different, and not as skippy as it was earlier. "What is wrong?"

"Ayen," she admitted. "I'll tell you later."

Alnor nodded warily and handed her a bow.

As she took it from his grasp, her eyes roamed around her surroundings to the other fighters. It wasn't busy yet, but that soon would change. She guessed everyone had been made aware of Naesaela's plan by now. They needed to be ready.

She glanced up, and for the first time, saw Mount Tejon in all its glory. She'd forgotten to ask Ayen to remove the shroud, but they must have sensed Alleria's need to see it. If it weren't for the circumstances, she could've awed at it all day, but she had to train. Forcing her gaze away, she removed an arrow from her quiver and aimed. It lurched from the bow and through the air. Alleria watched as it flew, and at the very last second, shot her hand forward. Light escaped her fingers and connected with the arrow. Then it was gone.

When she turned around, Aiwen and Tanyth were staring at her, mouth agape. Tanyth must have made his way over when he saw that she'd returned.

"You couldn't do that before," Tanyth stated the obvious.

"I've been training a lot. I can hone my power wherever I want now."

"It's incredible."

Alleria smiled, truly happy her friends were with her again. It hadn't sunk in. "Are you two training together?" She winked at the boys.

Aiwen and Tanyth stumbled over their words.

"Oh, no." Tanyth paused and then pointed. "I'm going to go over there."

Alleria opened her mouth to object, but Tanyth had already turned away and sauntered off. Confused, she turned to Aiwen to question his actions, but Aiwen shrugged and began to train again. She would question them later.

"Alleria, instead of standing around—"

"Ok, ok," Alleria interrupted. She laughed dryly and took her place.

Satisfied, Alnor went to turn but stopped. "Actually, I want you to train at Tanyth's tent."

"Tanyth's… why?"

"I don't know why it never occurred to me, but I want you to practise your power on something weightier and bigger. The heft and surface area of the weapon should do more damage, right?"

"I guess so," Alleria said, already placing the bow on the table. She retired the arrow in hand to her quiver and promptly set off to find Tanyth.

There were hundreds of stations on the training ground, but it didn't take long to spot his blonde curls, which were still as perfect as ever. She snuck behind him and pounced on his shoulders.

"Guess who."

"Hmmm, Alnor?"

Alleria slapped his head and jumped from his

shoulders. "I have been informed that I must practise with an axe."

Tanyth raised his brows. "I always knew you'd come to your senses. It is a much better weapon."

She shrugged. "Alnor's orders."

TANYTH PICKED A SIZEABLE AXE FROM THE TABLE and flung it toward Alleria. Luckily, she caught the handle and not the blade. She glared at him. "I love you, but that almost sliced my hand off."

"You can still do magic with one hand," Tanyth joked. He winked at her, and without looking, hauled an axe from the table and threw it toward the target. With a loud crash, it planted itself in the bullseye.

"Show off," Alleria scoffed.

"What can I say?"

She inspected the axe and its broad wooden handle. It was engraved with something, but seemed to be a language unknown to her. Or it was just heavily worn. Then she looked to Tanyth, wanting to know what the weird interaction with Aiwen was.

"What happened back there?"

Tanyth craned his neck, confused. But then it hit him. "Oh, that was nothing."

"Tanyth."

"I prom—"

"Tanyth..."

"Fine," he said, giving in. Alleria's stern tone always seemed to get him to cave. He hopped onto the table, and Alleria did the same. "Aiwen and I are having some issues. He's not ready for...." Tanyth motioned his hands in front of him, unsure how to word his sentence. *"This."*

Alleria threw him a crooked smile. "I'm sorry."

Tanyth shrugged, but his eyes rang differently. He was hurt, and the sadness oozing from him couldn't be hidden away and wrapped up tightly in a box. Feelings had to be shared and talked about. Alleria couldn't believe she didn't notice it before. "I was a bastard to him when he told me, but—"

"Look," Alleria said. "You have every right to be upset, too. You're both human. Maybe you overreacted, or whatever. But, it doesn't change that it hurt you, too. I know you, and I know you're blaming yourself for it all right now. For everything that went wrong."

Tanyth opened his mouth to speak.

"Am I wrong?" Alleria questioned.

He closed his mouth, shaking his head.

She wrapped her arm around his body and

leaned her head against his chest. "At the end of the day, you've been friends for much longer than you were together. That friendship would not break so easily. Eventually, you'll both get over what happened, and you'll come back stronger… I promise."

"It's easier said than done."

"Well, life is hard sometimes. Deal with it."

To Alleria's delight, Tanyth chuckled. "Alright, alright." He jumped from the table and snatched an axe. "Less relationship advice, more axe throwing."

She rolled her eyes and jumped off the table herself, accepting the axe from Tanyth as she did so. "We'll continue this conversation later!"

"Sure."

Alleria took her place before the target.

"Just relax," he said, clearly happy to change the subject.

She nodded, closed her eyes, and wiggled her body free of negative thoughts that tried and tried to cloud her mind. Then she pulled the axe back and launched it forward. When the thump sounded, she opened her eyes. The axe was planted in the ground only lengths away from her.

A great laugh erupted from Tanyth's throat. "You had to have a flaw, let's face it."

• • •

HOURS LATER, ALNOR MADE HIS WAY TO THEIR TENT.

"Alleria, let us see how you've progressed."

She took the axe in her hand and prepared her stance. She'd discovered she worked better with larger axes. There was more surface area for her magic to hit and, therefore, less of a chance to miss. *And* there'd be a more substantial gash if it did strike something. She dug her feet into the ground and pulled the axe behind her before throwing it forward. Instantly, as the axe left her grasp, she let the light escape her fingers.

Alnor watched, still shocked whenever she used her power, as the light joined with the axe. The weapon seemed to illuminate a shade of decadent gold before becoming one with the light, and the next thing they knew, it was flying past the valleys. "Well, let us hope no one is on the receiving end of that axe throw."

"She's still not great at the aiming part," Tanyth said. "But it'll do."

Alleria pushed him playfully. "Well, I'd like to see you shoot an arrow!"

"We are not talking about me, Alleria."

"If it weren't for the circumstances, I would so make you try."

"As would I," Alnor said. "Now, Alleria, if you—"

THE GROUND SHUDDERED. ALLERIA DIDN'T NEED TO ask what it was. She already knew. Naesaela's tenure of terror had begun.

"What do we do?" She yelled, her voice only just audible over the rumbles.

"Stick with me," Alnor said, already pacing toward the archery tent. Without turning back, he spoke again, "We'll get Aiwen, then get everyone in formation."

Alleria retrieved an axe from the table and looked toward Tanyth. He'd sheathed multiple on his breeches and one in his boot. When he was done, he peeked up and met Alleria's worried glare.

"It will be fine," he said, a pathetic attempt at reassurance. But it wasn't his fault. They were stepping into the unknown. No one knew how to act, or how to feel.

A tear pooled at Alleria's eye, threatening to tumble down her cheek. She'd bottled down her emotions all this time, but now it all felt real, and she couldn't hold it in. It wished to burst from within her, just like her spectacle at the town hall the day before. She was a hypocrite. She'd told

Tanyth to let his feelings out, but that was the opposite of what had done.

"But what if it isn't?" She said. "What if it isn't fine?"

Tanyth bit his lip. Nervous. "Then we'll go down together."

CHAPTER 30

"So much for training all day," Aiwen said as they reached his tent.

He stopped behind the table where he'd laid out bows for Alleria to choose and more arrows for her to add to her quiver. She plucked out the lightest, yet most beautiful bow, not wanting to carry too much weight, and refilled her quiver. The bow was new. Well, it at least looked like it. A deep mahogany with slight reds, but still brown. There were trees in Elorin almost the identical colour. That was why she chose this bow; it made her feel closer to home. It made her think of her mother. She wanted her by her side when she fought.

"You ok?" Alleria eventually asked.

"Is that a trick question?" Aiwen bent down

and removed a blade from his boot and handed it to Alleria. "Just in case."

"Aiwen, you need it—"

"You need it more." He forced her hands around the dagger, and she unwillingly sheathed it on her thigh. Aiwen beamed in success and shot Tanyth a momentary smile, which he surprisingly returned.

"Thank you," Alleria said. "Where did Alnor go?"

"He's rounding up everybody. We're meeting them all in the square."

"The square… why?"

"Biggest empty area… we can see everything around us there. It seemed the safest bet."

"Don't you think we'd be rather close to everyone? There are families—"

"Those who aren't fighting are being evacuated as we speak; if worse comes to worst, they can go to Innai. Alnor says, on horseback, it would take three hours at most."

Alleria scoffed. "It doesn't matter if they do or not. If we fail, we're all dead."

"Yes, but it's just insurance," Aiwen said, matching Alleria's tone.

"Alleria, he's right," Tanyth said. "Even if we do succeed, there's going to be carnage and havoc and… bloodshed. We want people who are not fighting as far away as possible because it will not be pretty around here."

It was all so much. Alleria's brain had gone to nothing but mush. Of course, it was the right idea. What was she thinking? Children couldn't be here during the attack. It was inhumane. They had to at least try to preserve their childhood before murder and destruction tainted it. If Alleria, of all people, had a happy childhood, they should too.

"You're right," she said finally. "I'm all over the place right now."

Aiwen huffed. "Get it together." He was already walking off as he spoke the harmful words, presumably to find Alnor.

Tanyth was as taken aback as Alleria.

"What is his problem?" Alleria asked.

"I think he's scared and just wants to go home. You know Aiwen, he likes structure in his life, and we haven't really had much of that recently."

"I get it."

"I think with that and," Tanyth pointed to himself. "It's just a lot for him."

Alleria nodded. "Well, let's do this, so we can get home."

"Hey, Al," Tanyth called as she turned away. She'd taken a few steps toward the square but froze when he spoke her name. She jerked her whole body around to face Tanyth again.

"What is it?" She said, clearly wanting to get to the others. Naesaela wouldn't wait.

Realising now wasn't the time, Tanyth pushed the thought to the back of his mind. He'd ask later. "I'll ask later—"

"No, I've got time," she countered. "We can talk on the way."

He nodded, and the pair made their way to the town square.

"Ok, shoot."

"Alright, this was just an observation, so you can't get mad." He raised his hands in innocence. "I saw you looking at Imra when we first got here. And you were rather flirty before you left to find Ayen."

INSTANTANEOUSLY, ALLERIA'S CHEEKS BURNED bright crimson. She brought her hands to her face to hide them. "I was curious as to who she was. Besides, I'm just a friendly person." Alleria straightened her posture to sell the lie. "I had never seen her before, so of course I'd look at her."

Tanyth chuckled to himself. "Alright, I believe you… so you don't think she's beautiful?"

"Well, I didn't say that—"

"Ha!" Tanyth jeered.

"What? She's a beautiful woman."

"Alleria." Tanyth truly looked at her. He knew her better than anyone.

Alleria caught his stare and struggled to fight his persuasive ways, but inevitably failed. "Fine!" She gave in. "I do like her!"

"I knew it."

"Well, yes, I like her. But I don't know her. I've said no more than fifty words to her."

"You can say a lot in fifty words, Alleria," Tanyth said. He smirked as if he had just recited the most brilliant thing ever written. But he was right. You didn't even need words to say a lot.

"TANYTH, I ASKED HER HOW SHE KNEW YOU. THAT is all." A smile crept onto her lips.

"That, among other things! Her dress for one of them—"

"That was purely an innocent compliment."

"In what world—"

"Tan, if I promise to speak to her when this is all over, will you please stop this?"

Tanyth nodded enthusiastically.

"Fine, I will." For a moment, her smile fell to a silent look of worry. Of sadness. Of the fear of rejection.

"What's wrong?"

"Nothing." She beamed, but it reeked of falsity.

Instantly, he shook his head, denying her claims. "The last thing you need right now are secrets. So, spill."

HE WAS RIGHT. THE TASK AT HAND REQUIRED HER complete focus. She couldn't risk being thrown off by her inner thoughts and struggles. *She was only human.*

"I don't know if she'd even want what I want," she blurted out. Alleria looked away, not wanting to see Tanyth's reaction when she finally admitted her secrets.

"How do you mean?" He reached for her face and turned her to face him. "Alleria, you know you can talk to me."

Her body trembled from the inside out. Why was she so nervous about speaking her truth? Tanyth was her best friend, not a stranger. "I don't know if I could ever see myself with someone—"

"Well, that's ok," he said, tracing his hand down her back, patting it for comfort.

"No, I can see myself with people romantically," She paused to rub her face, and delay what was coming. "But not for anything further. Maybe one day but…" Her voice trailed off. As soon as the words left her lips, she couldn't tell if she was pleased to have the weight off her shoulders or burdened to have shared her deepest secret. She was a fraud, always eager to listen to others' quarrels, but never brave enough to have someone listen to her own. She couldn't look directly at him, so instead, kept walking. The square was in view now, and she could see people lining up. It was getting all too real.

"ALLERIA, STOP, PLEASE." TANYTH GRABBED HER shoulder, stopping her in her tracks, and pulled her to look at him. Tanyth stared at her, sadness in his eyes. "I don't enjoy seeing you upset. I mean, look what it does to me." He rubbed his eyes, even though no tears were looming. It was the sentiment that counted. "You have no reason to be scared to talk to me about that sort of thing. Or anything, for that matter. I know it's hypocritical of me since Aiwen and I kept our relationship secret, but just know I'm always here for you. I'd never judge you."

Alleria sniffled and wiped her face. She nodded. "I know, it's silly."

"It's not silly. Not at all... It's human."

"Well, am I even human?" She laughed. She was so powerful. Could she even class herself on the same level as Aiwen and Tanyth? It sounded conceited, but it was a reasonable, and a legitimate, point.

"Alleria, you're more human than any of us. You kept us alive. You looked after us. You consoled us. Your heart is more pure than anyone in this damned town." He peered around him at the valleys that peeked through gaps in the roofs. "You got us to a place we didn't even think existed two weeks ago, all because you had hope. I don't know anything or anyone *more* humane."

ALLERIA FORCED A SMILE AT HIS WORDS. IT TRULY was a beautiful sentiment. Although, she didn't know how much of it she, herself, believed. But when Tanyth looped his arm in hers and guided her forward, she let him.

"Now, let's go before they start panicking

about your whereabouts. I do not want to get on the council's bad side."

Alleria laughed sincerely. Tanyth always knew how to lift her mood to make her feel herself again. As much as he'd hate to hear it, they wouldn't be here without him and Aiwen. Their teamwork had saved them once before, and she just prayed to the Light, it would do the same again.

CHAPTER 31

Until now, Alleria didn't realise how many people lived in Aralva. The training ground was never this busy, so she assumed more citizens must have come forward to fight. The notion made her smile: that people admired their home enough to risk their lives for its safety. It was admirable.

The town square was a myriad of heights, shapes, culture and even species she didn't even recognise. She still hadn't had the chance to learn more about any of them, or even the chance to explore the markets and other ways of life. For that, she kicked herself. She shuffled through the crowds, glad the bustle and noise hid her from prying eyes. Everything was all too much already and being recognised would add another thing to worry about to the ever-growing list. Luckily, evacuations were still taking place, and the screams of children yearning for their parents distracted people enough not to notice her.

AFTER MUCH STRUGGLE, THE PAIR MANAGED TO carve a path through to Alnor. He stood with Ruven and the rest of the council, who settled just a few steps back. She didn't know for sure if Ruven was in charge, but it seemed pretty clear he was. The others never seemed to talk, but then again, she'd only met them once before, and she didn't stick around any longer than she needed to.

"Where have you been?" Alnor asked as they entered his visible vicinity. When Alleria didn't answer, he swiftly replaced his train of thought. "I've sent Aiwen to the archer's formation. It'll be safest there for him. Tanyth you go to—"

THE GROUND SHOOK AGAIN.

Nothing.

"That was—"

And again.

• • •

ALLERIA FELL TO THE FLOOR, FLINCHING AS HER knees made contact with the stone below. She glanced around her. Others had fallen, too. If Naesaela could make this many fall with just a quake, only the Light knows what she could do when she's free.

Sudden gasps caught Alleria's attention, but it wasn't until she rose to her feet that she saw why. All their faces turned behind her. She took a deep breath and rotated in her place. She heard them, but she saw what they were all gawking at. Rocks fell. The mountain was breaking.

"FORMATIONS!" Alnor screamed, attempting to capture everybody's attention. Luckily, it worked. Those who were still on the ground rose in seconds and ran to their places. It was hectic, but nobody faltered. Soon, everyone was in place.

From the corner of her eye, Alleria spotted Aiwen at the front line with the rest of the archers. At first, she worried for him, but she soon remembered that once he had fired the first arrows, he'd be towards the back of the fight, further from harm's way. It wasn't perfect, but it would have to do. She couldn't ask him to evacuate. He wouldn't do it, anyway. The thought of Imra suddenly penetrated her mind.

"Where is Imra?"

"Safe," Alnor said quickly, clearly not wanting to think about it too much. She was his niece, after all. Noticing his abrupt tone, and Alleria's worried glances, he turned to Alleria and continued. "I instructed her to evacuate when the time came. I haven't seen her since I left for the training grounds earlier today."

"That's good." Alleria stayed with Tanyth, awaiting instruction. After her display in the town hall, Ruven was still hesitant around Alleria.

"Alleria, are you ready?" Ruven asked. She wanted to laugh at the absurdity of his question.

"Do you want a genuine answer to that?"

"I want to know if I should expect the worst."

THE WORDS HIT HARD. PEOPLE DIDN'T NECESSARILY *not* believe in her, but they couldn't hide their apprehension. She didn't even know if she could do it. This whole time it foretold she could, that she will. But how did they know for sure? Yes, she was powerful. But was she powerful enough? She heard the sharp sounds of rocks falling behind her but didn't turn. It would only stress her even more.

"I feel strong," Alleria said. She straightened her posture in an attempt to convince him. They had their differences, but she knew low morale was the worst thing for a battle. They needed everyone at their top form, and if she had to lie to get that. She would. "I'll do this."

Ruven forced a nod, still unconvinced, and gestured to Alnor. "Make sure everyone has a weapon. And if people still haven't evacuated... make them fight."

Alnor shot Alleria a dismayed glance, following his words.

"You want them to fight?" Alleria croaked.

"We need the people."

"Ruven, there are children—"

"Enough," he interrupted, silencing her with his hands. "We have to face the harsh reality here. The people evacuating are just prolonging the inevitable. If we lose, we are all dead."

Alleria knew it was true, but it still felt wrong, heartless. At least, give people a chance. She opened her mouth to contest but was met with the same silencing hand. Her stomach knotted, but she unravelled it right away. She had to clear her mind, let her feelings float away. Now wasn't the time for this. "Where do you want me?"

. . .

"ALLERIA," A VOICE CALLED FROM BEHIND HER.

She jerked her head back to find Gaelin creeping towards her. He seemed to have aged even more since she last saw him. Despite the commotion, he didn't seem panicked like the rest of Aralva. "Before you fight, I must give you something."

"What is it?" she asked.

"My staff." Gaelin presented it to her, the power still radiating power in front of her.

"No, I couldn't—"

"Alleria, take it."

Gaelin forced the staff forward and into her hands. As it collided with her fingers, she felt a spark travel through her, as if the staff had chosen her. Everything suddenly felt right. She was proficient in various weapons, but this was different. With the staff, her power radiated stronger, brighter. She ran her gaze down the staff, following the dents it had gained over the years. The history it had witnessed. But now, she was history.

THE GROUND SHOOK AGAIN, AND INSTEAD OF THE now familiar sound of tumbling rocks. Screeches.

Everyone darted their heads to the mountain.

At first, confusion struck them all. Everything was blurry through a cold layer of fog. That was until the screeches got closer. Dark creatures had escaped the mountain's clutch. Naesaela's army. Of course, she had an army—she had thousands of years to prepare.

"Do not break my staff," Gaelin said and then disappeared into the bustle of people. He was old, and she didn't know how much help he would be. She hadn't even asked if he could use his magic without his weapon.

THE CROWDS COMPACTED AROUND HER, ALL readying for battle. Tanyth had been pushed away from her, but his blonde locks still bobbed above the rest. She convinced herself that he would be ok. He was the best fighter she knew. Before all hell broke loose, she darted her gaze toward the frontline in search of Aiwen, but it was no use. Hundreds of people and creatures stood before her, blocking her view.

The beastly screams grew louder and louder until the sources were within firing range. She couldn't see them aiming, but she saw the arrows flying. Some direct hits. Some misses. But the creatures did not fall. They flew closer and closer.

Alleria realised they were the creatures from her nightmare, the creatures that almost killed her. Winged beasts, a shade of black. Purple. Blue. She couldn't tell. The panic of the crowd distracted her too much. She needed to get out. She needed to reach higher ground because she couldn't risk using her power in the crowd. Just in case.

Gripping the aged staff with all her might, she pressed through the crowds. She burrowed her borrowed weapon into her chest and ran. Yells and screams overcame her senses, but she fought through the overwhelming noise.

Suddenly, bodies around her began to be plucked up by the devilish creatures, and moments later, were dropped like pieces of meat to the hard ground below. Dead. She craved to stop and help every single person, but time was against her. If she didn't reach higher ground, she wouldn't able to help anyone.

Closing her eyes to mask the death, Alleria just ran. She barged into many but persisted. Now was not the time to apologise. Eventually, the crowds dwindled, and she found herself on the outskirts of the fight, beside a tall wagon. She knew what to do. Instantly, she ran over to it and scaled the wooden vehicle. It wasn't as high as she would've liked, but it would have to do. Then… she saw.

. . .

BODIES PILED ON THE FLOOR. THE ARCHERS HADN'T had a chance to retreat before Naesaela's creatures attacked. Scattered across the floor, they were lifeless, weapons still in hand, determination still frozen on their face. They fought til their last breath. Alleria had to do the same. She owed them that much. Her eyes darted across the cadavers for any sign of Aiwen, but his slim frame wasn't among those dead. She felt her mind slipping. Clamping her eyes shut, she tried to block out the world for a moment. Breathe. Her oncoming wave of terror subsided for a moment, but soon returned in full force when the screams grew closer. She needed to do something, and quick. Her eyes shot open again.

Cementing her feet into the wooden floor, she leaned into herself and her power. She aimed Gaelin's staff toward the sky, and before she knew it, the seal inside her was shattering. She felt the warmth of power in her stomach boiling inside her, travelling through her body and into her fingertips. The red jewel morphed into a deep gold before her eyes. It rumbled beneath her tight grip, challenging her strength, but she did not waver. She pushed the staff forward, and an arc of golden light shot from the gem, so bright it almost blinded her. Squinting, she tried to look past the blast, but to no avail. She could only hear the screeches of the beasts deafening before melting to a slight whimper. And then nothing.

FORCING THE STAFF DOWN, THE POWER RETREATED, and her eyes could once again see the battlefield. The winged beasts were gone, the only remnants of them being burnt ashes that gracefully sank to the ground. It reminded her of the library, of the feather and the storm. Of the time before this.

Cheers erupted from the crowds, but Alleria's face didn't change. It wasn't over. This was just the start.

By the time she'd descended the wagon, the screeches sounded once more. She hesitated for a moment, her foot still teetering on the vehicle, but eventually brought it to the ground. She couldn't use her power repeatedly. She needed to preserve it for what was to come. With a mighty groan, Alleria reentered the bustling crowds. There were fewer people now. When she looked down, she knew why. Fallen soldiers taken too soon, too young. She wanted to kneel beside each one and pray they make it to the other side, but she pressed the urge away. Scrunching her face, she pushed through. Stumbling led to running, and eventually, she made it to the front of the formation. Archers lay dead all around her, their faces cemented in horror. She kneeled beside one man, his eyes clawed out and torso bloody. She kissed her hand and placed it on his head. "May you have peace."

SOON, HEADS TURNED AS PEOPLE REALISED ALLERIA had joined the front lines. Everyone fell silent. Yet, the screeches still sounded somewhere beyond the clouds. They couldn't see the beasts yet, but they were coming. Alleria spun to find every soldier's eyes on her. She spotted Aiwen and Tanyth standing on the wagon she'd been standing on. Thank the Light they were ok. She needed to say something. They were waiting for her instruction because they trusted her. People at the back had propped themselves up to see. Surely, the saviour knew what to do. Alleria brushed her callused hands through her now sweat-filled hair, picking the loose strands from her face.

She coughed, ensuring her throat was clear, and raised her voice. "We have lost many already!" She yelled. "We've lost mothers, fathers, sons, daughters, and friends. But enough is enough."

A few small cheers sounded infrequently throughout the crowd. But the rest stayed silent, some with tears in their eyes for their fallen family. They lost people they'd known their entire lives, and Alleria had only known them but a few days. But she knew how they felt. How it felt for *your* person to be ripped away without a goodbye in such a brutal and tragic way. It wasn't fair.

"My power needs to be reserved for Naesaela—"

Sudden gasps interrupted Alleria. She'd forgotten how much fear was bestowed in that name.

"Naesaela is not a name to be feared. Naesaela is a coward who hides behind mind control, illusions, and deceptions. However, I cannot deny her power, and I must reserve my power for her." Alleria paced back and forth, the screeches sounding closer and closer. "We have little time, but you must know. The only way to kill these beasts is a strike through the eye or removing their heads. Naesaela's magic will protect them from any other attack… trust me, I know."

She flicked her gaze to Aiwen, whose hand was resting on his laceration. She'd be lying if she said she wasn't scared. They'd only just survived the wolf attack, let alone winged beasts and

Naesaela herself. Only two weeks ago, Alleria was working in the library, unbeknownst to Aralva at all. Now, she was expected to save it and the rest of Malmar. Everything rested on her shoulders, but she would need everyone's help to succeed.

Alleria spun around at the close sound of screeches. Her gaze met the beasts just as they appeared through the grey clouds. They dove straight toward them. Dropping Gaelin's staff to the floor, she pulled the bow from her back and aimed.

"AIM!" SHE FOCUSED HER ARROW DIRECTLY AT ONE creature and followed its erratic flight path to a tee, not wanting to waste an arrow and miss her shot. She couldn't afford to miss. "FIRE!"

A slew of arrows flew from all around the battlefield. This time, beasts dropped from the sky and splatted to the cold ground below. Their aim was better, but not perfect. Beasts still rushed straight for them. Cheers erupted but were cut short by Alleria's shouts.

"AGAIN.... FIRE!"

More arrows sliced through the brisk air, and the last of the beasts fell. But Alleria did not lower her weapon and was glad she didn't when the ground rumbled again. But this time it was different. It was stronger. It was…

She dug her heels into the ground and didn't let herself falter.

It was happening, and she couldn't stop it.

Naesaela was coming.

CHAPTER 32

The blast threw everyone back.

BURNT AIR SUFFOCATED ALLERIA'S SENSES AND distorted her vision. Mist surrounded them. It was all a blur. Clambering to her feet, Alleria winced. The mountain's rubble had grazed her uncovered skin and blood trickled down her arms. Luckily, the staff was still beside her, but her bow was nowhere to be seen. It would have to do. She felt for her axe, but it must have slipped away in the blast. She only had the staff, and if her power depleted… she was defenseless. The sound of silence thundered in her ears. She didn't notice Tanyth calling her name until he and Aiwen were at her side. He shook her gently to check she was ok.

"Alleria." His voice was quiet, but she could hear him now, even if it was faint. "Are you ok?"

She acknowledged him with a nod, and for the first time, let her eyes glaze over everyone else. Many people leapt to their feet, but hundreds still lied fallen. She couldn't tell if they were unconscious or dead. Panicked, she shot her gaze back to the boys.

"You need to get out of here," she snapped.

"No—"

"Please—"

"Alleria, no." Aiwen yelled. Fury lashed behind his hazel eyes, but for a good reason. He stood his ground and would not let her talk them out of helping. "We have made it this far together. You are not doing this alone… You said so yourself - we are stronger as a family."

He was right, but the bodies that slumped around them required her to think differently. What kind of friend would she be if she willingly sent them to their deaths? Aiwen caught her troubled glances at the bodies and pulled her focus back.

"Alleria, we might very well die helping you… but we will definitely die if we don't." His voice rung softer, more caring as he spoke the words. Alleria lowered her head in understanding and pulled them both into an embrace.

"I love you both. I just don't want anything to happen to you."

"Nothing will," Tanyth said.

Pulling away, Alleria smiled. "Let's do this."

ALLERIA GRIPPED THE STAFF HARD, KNOWING THIS was her only chance. She had nothing left. As she turned, the mist departed, finally revealing the wreck of Mount Tejon. It bursted open. But she was nowhere to be seen. Alleria stepped back, allowing the boys to stand beside her. She embraced their warmth and suddenly felt stronger with them by her side. Aiwen had drawn his bow and Tanyth his axe. They were ready to put up a fight, even if it might be their last.

Suddenly, a violent wind shot from inside the mountain, causing the trio to step back. But as Alleria looked to the sky, she realised it wasn't a wind.

It was Naesaela.

Her black wings spanned for lengths upon lengths, casting an imposing shadow over the entire town square. Gasps and horrified cries overcame her senses as the surviving soldiers fled from the battlefield. Alleria wanted to yell for their return, but there was little they could do now. Hundreds had died, and they did not want to be next. She couldn't blame them.

An enormous roar filled the air as Naesaela circled Aralva, her wings sending large gusts of wind that stole their breath. Her frame was more considerable than any of them could have expected.

"HOLY SHIT," TANYTH SAID.

"Holy shit, indeed," Alleria replied, her knuckles turning white from her tightened grip on the staff. It reverberated with power beneath her grasp, ready for the moment to release.

"How do we even kill that thing?"

"I do not know," she said honestly. "But we will try, for I don't know what will happen if we don't."

Just then, Alnor appeared at their side. He hadn't left. He was the only one to stay. Alleria smiled but did not take her focus off of the circling dragon above them.

"Do we have a plan?" Alnor asked, aiming his bow.

"No," Aiwen said.

Alnor couldn't help but laugh nervously. "Great."

As Naesaela circled the group, they instinctively formed a circle. Their eyes didn't leave the beast for one moment. The flurries of wind became stronger and stronger... she was lowering to the ground. But suddenly, Naesaela burst into a dive with her mouth opened. Fire spewed from inside of her, directly toward them. Alleria jumped forward and raised the staff upward. The latch inside of her clicked open, and an outpouring of light enveloped them. A barricade of gold formed around the four, and as the fire came into contact with it, it fizzled out. With a roar, Naesaela landed some lengths away.

Alleria reluctantly lowered the staff, not wanting to use all of her power. She needed to be wise. She couldn't keep the shield up forever, as much as she'd like to. Forcing the staff down, she stood defiantly, as did the others. They did not falter their firm stance as Naesaela took a step forward. The ground convulsed with every impact on ground. Now she was close, Alleria realised her scales were not black like she had thought, but a dark evening purple. Enormous teeth protruded from her gnarly mouth, and her eyes leaked with the same purple as the wolves before. Alleria wanted to scream, but she repressed her fear. Instead, she readjusted the staff in her hand, making certain she'd be able to drive it forward when she needed to.

A DEEP SNICKER ESCAPED NAESAELA. THE SOUND sent a mind-deafening hum through the air. "Puny humans," she said, scowling at the four with their weapons aimed. "Your weapons cannot harm me."

Alleria bit her lip. "Naesaela—"

"Ah, the saviour is not scared to say my name. That is… refreshing." Her voice was deep and booming. She didn't know what she expected a dragon to sound like, but it wasn't this.

She wanted to cover her ears when she spoke, but she didn't. Standing her ground, she didn't want to reveal her intimidation.

"What do you want?" Alleria asked, putting her left foot forward. She tried to subdue Naesaela. Tanyth attempted to pull her back, but she wiggled free. "Why destroy Malmar?"

Another hum sounded in the air, a laugh so deep it didn't resemble one at all.

"You do not scare me… Alleria." Her voice was full of breath and hearing her name from Naesaela's mouth sent a shiver down her spine. She never spoke her name.

"How did you know that?" Alleria asked, her forehead crinkled.

"Know what, human?"

"My name."

SUDDENLY, NAESAELA SHOT FORWARD UNTIL HER old, scaled face was lengths away from Alleria's. "You think I am weak?" She roared. "I have my ways, Alleria. Do you really think I wouldn't know the name of the one who is destined to kill me?"

Somehow, the dragon's face displayed a smirk, and before their eyes, it suddenly changed. Naesaela's frame shrunk. They watched in confusion as the scales disappeared and her skin lightened. After a few moments, she was no longer a dragon on the outside. She was a humanoid. Pointed ears protruded from long blonde hair, and the scaly skin was replaced with long, luxurious robes.

Ayen.

. . .

THEY ALL STEPPED BACK, SEEMINGLY MORE ALARMED by what happened than the dragon that stood in its place seconds before.

"Alleria Valrona, it is so lovely to see you again."

"What… how?" She said, her heart pounding out of her chest.

"You must hear yourself." Ayen laughed. "Who would have thought the saviour would be so… scared."

Alleria shook her head and even debated pinching her skin. Surely not. Surely, Ayen was not Naesaela all this time? Why would an elf go against their beliefs, their principles. Go against what makes them elves? "Ayen… why?"

With that, Ayen crept closer until their face met Alleria's, and only a brief gap separated them. A short guffaw left their perfect lips before speaking. "Alleria Valrona, you are mistaken. I murdered that puny elf weeks ago."

MIND REELING, ALLERIA FALTERED BACK, ONLY TO be caught by Alnor's firm grasp. His face was just as horror-struck as Alleria. Ayen was the one to get her here in the first place… she only spoke to them early that day. They seemed so real. Her whole life had been a lie, and now the last few weeks had been too. She felt her power sizzling inside her, imploding under the weight of the revelations, just demanding clemency.

"So when I spoke to Ayen the first time…" Her voice trailed out as she slowly put things together.

A smile seemed permanently plastered on Ayen's — Naesaela's face. "That was I. I tried to control you like you have seen me do to so many, but I could not pass through your magical barriers. So I had to resort to intercepting your power… I must admit, I wasn't expecting the ice, but when opposites collide, something strange is bound to happen—"

"You're a monster."

"Anyway," Naesaela barked. "I realised then that you were too strong to be killed from afar. So I murdered Ayen and intercepted your dreams instead. That way, I could kill you myself."

Alleria shook her head, not wanting to believe the subterfuge she'd fallen for. It didn't add up correctly. "How could you have possibly killed Ayen?" Alleria said. "You were trapped!"

Glaring down, *Naesaela* replied. "Alleria, I am growing tired of these endless questions."

Alleria's stance didn't move. She would rather die than not find out the truth. She owed that much to Ayen, even if she never actually met them.

Eventually, Naesaela gave in. "I have been strong enough for months, but I am patient. I waited until I knew of your location—"

"That doesn't answer my question," Alleria said.

"Alleria, careful," Aiwen whispered, pulling her back.

"Listen to your pathetic friends, Alleria."

"Tell me what I asked," she persisted.

Naesaela grinned. "Well, you would think it would be tougher to control some elves."

THEIR EYES WIDENED IN SHOCK, BUT SOON TURNED to resentment. Alleria felt like her heart would fail from beating so hard, so fast. Other elves had murdered Ayen. His own family had taken his life, and they didn't even know. Fury boiled in Alleria's veins. How could someone—something have been so heartless, so—

Suddenly, Alleria lurched forward, not thinking about the consequences. As she moved, she retrieved an axe from Tanyth's boot and hurled it forward. The cool metal sliced through the air before bouncing off Naesaela's frame. It hit the floor with a smash, and Alleria watched as it shattered into thousands of pieces. At that moment, Naesaela swung her arm forward, knocking Alleria to the floor. Tanyth and Aiwen ran to her side and helped her to her feet. When they looked back up, Ayen's slim frame was gone; Naesaela had returned to her proper form. Giant shadows cascaded over them all, sending everything around them into a false darkness. Alnor hadn't moved from where they stood before and seemingly disappeared into the shroud of darkness.

"It is your time to die, Alleria," Naesaela said. "Your friends too."

The ground shook violently, catching them off guard. They stumbled around to keep balance, and when their eyes met with Naesaela again, her mouth was open. The fire was seething inside her, lighting her up from the inside out. Surrounding them in a barrier of light, Alleria raised her arms, allowing the Light to protect them. A familiar scream sounded from their left as the fire escaped Naesaela's giant mouth. Suddenly, large hands collided with the barrier, and Alnor's face appeared beside them. Alleria's heart dropped, for she couldn't release the barrier without killing them all. In a desperate attempt to live, Alnor pushed his hands against the cold floor, and absorbed the stone. But it was not enough. It was not enough to fight off the blaze. It protected him for a moment, but the stone soon blackened under the flares. All they could do was watch as the flames encircled the barrier of light, and Alnor turned to ash before their eyes. Soon his guttural screams were no more than a recent memory and Alnor was dead.

FIGHTING THE IMPULSE TO LOWER HER ARMS, Alleria pushed her sorrow deep into her chest. Now was not the time to mourn, because Aiwen and Tanyth's lives depended on it. She stiffened her arms, reinforcing the barrier and resisting the flames' growing heat. But soon, it became unbearable. All the boys could do was watch as Alleria struggled. Tanyth and Aiwen eyed each other, and for that moment, it felt like nothing ever happened between them. They were just two men, friends for the entirety of their lives . Their differences were a thing of the past, and they were going to die together.

"I'm sorry!" Alleria yelled, trying to make herself heard over the conflagrations. "I'm sorry for dragging you both into this."

Aiwen stepped forward. "Alleria, we chose to be here."

"And I shouldn't have allowed that—"

Alleria stumbled back as her power diminished. They all stood paralysed as the shield faded to a pale yellow. It was about to break. She rounded to her friends, insisting they join her side. Death was unknown, but Alleria didn't fear it. She feared losing the ones she loved, but death itself was natural. Without question, the boys took their place on either side of her and huddled close. She relished with the fact she would die beside the ones she loved, only wishing her mother was with her. Yes, she ached for the lives of her friends, but if she had sent them away, and she died, they would still die soon after. There was no easy way out or path to cheat Naesaela's plan. At least, this way… they were together. Till the end. Tanyth took her face in his hands and turned her focus to him.

"Let go, Alleria. We're ready."

HIS WORDS ECHOED IN HER HEAD AS SHE GAVE INTO Naesaela's power. Dropping her arms to her side, the flames encapsulated them, circling them as the last remnants of the Light protected them. The heat rose with every second, and their skin boiled beneath its warmth. As the power dissipated, she took Aiwen's hand in her right and Tanyth's in her left. She let her eyes flit closed. Her time was over, and her power was diminished. A prophecy was foretold, but not always true. Time was fluid, and things changed; sometimes for the better, and sometimes—

THE FIRE WITHDREW.

They all shot their gazes toward Naesaela, who was stumbling back, roaring in pain. Then they saw. A winged creature circled the battlefield; its screeches cut through Naesaela's roars. Alleria watched in awe at the sight, and as it lowered to the ground, she recognised the creature. Vaalyun flew through the air with grace and pose, and as he turned, she spotted the rider. Imra. She'd returned. Suddenly, hundreds of silhouettes appeared in the skyline, approaching with haste. As they drew closer, Rosa's compact frame came into view on the back of Nephinae. Hundreds of creatures followed Rosa tightly, and at that moment, Alleria realised they were from the menagerie. After twenty years, they were all free. They returned to Aralva. Squealing, she took Aiwen and Tanyth's hands and ran toward Imra and Rosa, touching down on the ground. The rest of the creatures circled the battlefield, ready to attack.

Alleria wrapped her arms around Rosa as soon as she stepped onto Aralvan soil. "You came," she cried.

Rosa pointed a finger toward her daughter. "Thanks to Imra… where's Alnor?"

Her mouth gaped. Alleria looked at Rosa, her hands balled into a fist at the thought of it still. There was nothing she could have done, even so, she blamed herself. At that moment, Rosa understood Alleria's hesitance, and Imra fell to her knees. Screaming, she ripped grass from the soil. Tanyth knelt beside her and pulled her into his chest, muffling the cries.

"I'm sorry," Alleria said. "It's all my—"

"No," Rosa interrupted, raising her finger. "It is no one's fault but that monster's."

THEY ALL SPUN TO WHERE NAESAELA LIED, STILL writhing in pain.

"What did you do to her?" Aiwen asked.

Imra brushed her hair from her face and got to her feet. Her eyes were bloodshot, and tears still poured down her face. "Arrows made from the dawn wood. The same wood the pyre she was burnt on was made of."

"How did you know it would work?"

"It was a guess." Imra reached into the bag on her side and pulled a handful of arrows from inside. They were light brown, almost beige. They'd been carved into the arrow shape but were imperfect, not perfectly smooth. Imra closed the distance between herself and Alleria before placing the arrows in her hands. She wrapped her hand in Alleria's and whispered. "This is your fight. Do my uncle proud."

"I will," Alleria replied. She placed the arrows in her quiver, all but one. She twirled it between her fingers for a moment and then turned to her friends. "Too many people have died… this ends now. Rosa, will the other creatures help?"

Rosa nodded. "They won't be as strong as your arrows, but they can provide a distraction."

"That will have to do." Turning to Aiwen and Tanyth, she crumpled her brow. "There is no point in telling you to leave, is there?"

They both shook their heads in defiance, but smirks appeared on their faces.

"Very well… please don't die."

"Not planning on it," Tanyth said.

Alleria turned back to Naesaela and dropped the staff to her feet, the weapon now useless for their cause. She reached her hand out, and Aiwen instinctively placed his bow in her grasp. Inclining her head in gratitude, she gripped the wooden longbow in her worn hands and traced her fingers over its smooth grooves. Archery was her strong suit, where she felt free. Now, she just hoped it was enough.

CHAPTER 33

"That was quite the show," Naesaela said as she heaved her colossal frame from the frigid ground. "It is too bad you will not live to see the encore."

The arrow disorientated her for a moment, but its effect didn't seem to last for too long. She was weaker, but still towered over them with ease like she could crush them by just lifting one scaly claw. Just noticing the creatures above her, a chuckle escaped her gnarly mouth.

"Well, I must say, you have outdone yourselves. This is quite the spectacle, and it's all for me!" Naesaela lowered her glare from the sky and pursued Alleria. Her steps sent thunderous shakes across the square. It took all their might not to flounder at the impact.

"Stay back," Alleria said, her voice raised. She stumbled the arrow into place and aimed. "I will shoot."

Craning her neck, Naesaela froze in place, halting the minute earthquakes that came with each stomp. "It is no use, Alleria—"

"NO," Alleria roared, stepping closer to the beast. She pulled the bow string tighter, threatening to snap under the force of her grasp. "You have taken *so* much from me, and I will not let you take *anything* or *anyone* else." Her words were full of hurt and hatred, and with one quick movement, she let go of the arrow. It sliced through the air and hurtled straight for Naesaela's head. Everything fell mute, bar the quiet sound of the arrow whipping through the air. However, inches away from her face, Naesaela ducked with much needed haste, and the arrow glided straight past her. A guttural scream left Alleria's chapped lips.

NOW CROUCHED, NAESAELA LUNGED FORWARD, HER claws outstretched for Alleria's throat. Fiddling with her quiver, she tried to pull another arrow, but wasn't quick enough. She launched into a roll, only missing the dragon by a few lengths. Screams of her name overcame her senses but were soon blocked out when her head hit the floor. Disorientated, she gestured for her friends to run, scared Naesaela would turn to them whilst she was down. Alleria stumbled to her feet and didn't look back.

Instantly, Naesaela turned to Alleria, and hurled herself toward her again. Jumping out of the way, Alleria narrowly missed the dragon's ferocious snap. While Naesaela was turned, she swiftly pulled an arrow from her quiver. Her eyes widened, surprised it was still intact from the countless bashes with the floor. With haste, she aimed the arrow and let go just as Naesaela turned her body back around. The dragon ducked, but the arrow skimmed her back, sending a spur of blood into the air. A thundering roar escaped her mouth, but she did not fall. It wasn't deep enough.

"If only you were a good shot," Naesaela stepped forward. "You could have killed me, and this would *all* be over." She stepped again.

But Alleria didn't falter as the steps rattled the ground.

"Now… You will die, your friends too. And then the rest of Aralva. And then—"

Her words were cut short when something swiped at Naesaela's face. It whipped in the wind, back and forth, slicing all the way down the dragon's body. Alleria took no time in waiting and ran to get some distance between herself and the creature. She retrieved another arrow as she sprinted away. When she finally turned back, she saw her mystery saviour. It wasn't one. It was two. Vaalyun and Nephinae, conducted by Imra and Rosa, took one last swipe at Naesaela before launching back into the air. Naesaela fell to the ground in torment, but it wouldn't last. They were only surface wounds.

WITH ALACRITY, ALLERIA FIRED THE DAWN WOOD arrow. She didn't aim it with precision, just her dwindling hope. As it flew, she felt a familiar warmth inside of her; instinctively, she dropped the bow and lurched her hands forward. Bolts of light shot from each palm, before fusing itself with the arrow, just as it made contact with Naesaela's slumped frame. The roars were unbearable as the arrow lodged itself in the dragon's side.

Alleria pulled her hands back, confused about what had just happened. She flexed her fingers, but nothing else came. Her power had come back in a time of need but diminished once again. She threw her hands to her side, picked up the bow, and stormed forward. This ended now. As she approached Naesaela, Tanyth and Aiwen fortified their friendship. They hadn't run away like she'd told them to. But they were safe. That was all that mattered. They took place beside Alleria.

"That was incredible," Tanyth said as he draped his arms around her. He squeezed her like it was his last. As if he thought he'd lost her. Pulling away, he spoke louder. "Imra and Rosa are still somewhere up there." He pointed upward, a smile setting on his lips.

"You had us worried," Aiwen said.

Alleria turned to him and laughed. "It would be boring if there wasn't a bit of a chase."

Rolling his eyes, Aiwen turned to Naesaela. She was unconscious, but it was only a matter of time before she awoke again, as strong as before.

"What's the plan now?" Tanyth asked as he strode toward the sleeping dragon. He bent his legs to get a better look at the creature in awe of her aged face. Close up, her dark purple scales were flecked with black, and seemingly rotting. Turning around, he spoke again. "Will another arrow do it?"

Alleria shrugged. "One in the eye, I hope." She removed the final arrow from her quiver and flipped it in her hands. "Ready to end this, and go home?"

Aiwen nodded. "More than ready."

"I thought you'd never—"

Tanyth stopped talking, his sentence abrupt and unfinished as his face paled in horror-stricken. Then his eyes bulged and his mouth gaped. A hissing of air escaped his mouth, but no words.

Furrowing his brow, Aiwen tutted. "Can you be serious for once, Tan—"

A RIP TORE THROUGH THE QUIET SQUARE.

CHAPTER 34

Confusion was their initial reaction, then realisation.

Alleria screamed first.

Then Aiwen.

Naesaela had pierced Tanyth's stomach from back to front. Her soaked talon dripped blood to the stone floor below, staining it a sickening red. Time slowed as the dragon retracted her claw through his still frame, leaving a giant hole in its wake.

Tanyth fell to the floor with a thud.

CHAPTER 35

Dropping the bow, Alleria's scream of terror turned to rage. She gripped the arrow tightly and launched herself toward Naesaela. Still weak, the dragon didn't move, and didn't fight when Alleria hurled the arrow through her eye and into her brain. Instead, her head dropped to the ground, and the light behind her eyes vanished. The evil was dead.

Aiwen sunk to his former lover's side, his guttural screams now but a heavy whimper. Tears streamed down his face as he tried to stop the bleeding, his hands acting like a human bandage against the wound. He lowered his face to Tanyth's, whose eyes were frozen in place, the shock of the situation still settling in. Coos of reassurance left Aiwen's lips. "It'll be ok, Tan," he whispered as he propped up his limp head on his lap. His eyes flickered with the sweet lure of death. Aiwen shot his gaze to Alleria just as she pulled the arrow from the dragon's eye. His voice raised, he turned back to Tanyth. "We need to get him a healer or—"

Alleria placed her hand on his shoulder. "Aiwen, it's no use—"

"You do not tell me what is no use. We need to get him out of here to find a healer."

"Aiwen." Alleria knelt down to his level. A tear escaped her duct; threatening to spill down her cheek. "We must use this time to make him feel comfortable. He's finally with his closest friends in an evil free land. Let's make this worth it for him."

The whimpers turned to cries and eventually wails. "But—"

"I know," was all Alleria said as she held Aiwen in her arms. "I know… come on, say what you want to Tanyth."

Nodding, he shuffled out of Alleria's warm embrace. Despite the fading light in his eyes, Aiwen and Tanyth caught each other's glance. At that moment, it was just them. They were back together in Elorin, still sneaking around, loving in silence. They didn't care. They couldn't show affection in public because they were together.

They were alive. Young and innocent, their only worries caught in rainfall during work. It was a beautiful tale, perfect even, but all stories had to end, eventually. That was why they were stories and not reality. Stories were fabricated in the best version of a person. Reality was honest and brutal in truth.

"Hey Tan, can you hear me?" Aiwen whispered, his face inches from his lover's. He wanted to scream for the whole of Aralva to hear, but knew peace was what Tanyth deserved. And he would give him that, even if it broke his heart. "It's me, and Alleria… you're going to be ok, my beautiful boy."

Lowering his bloodstained hand, Aiwen reached for Tanyth's. He placed it in his lifeless palm, just to feel him for the last time. The icy touch made him flinch, but he didn't cry. Instead, a gasp left Aiwen's lips when he felt a slight tug at his fingers. Tanyth's fingers intertwined with his own, and his lips twitched to utter something, but nothing escaped.

"It's ok, you don't need to talk," Aiwen said, his other hand cupping Tanyth's cold cheek. "You're the one who taught me you don't need to say anything to say a lot. This right here." He eyed their hands. "This tells me all I need to know… I love you, Tanyth, and Alleria does, too. We always will."

They both looked into Tanyth's eyes for a hint of emotion, but nothing came. Aiwen turned to Alleria, "Do you think I could have a moment alone with him?"

"Of course," she said. Reaching down, she planted a kiss on his forehead. "Good night, Tanyth," she whispered through faint cries. "Thank you for making the hard days easier and the easy days nothing but a breeze." She kissed his forehead again, not wanting to let go, before eventually clambering to her feet. She nodded to Aiwen and then set off to find Imra and Rosa.

"IT'S JUST US TWO AGAIN," AIWEN SAID. HE HADN'T let go of Tanyth's hand. He didn't think he could, not now; not yet. Tears formed in his eyes. They balled before bursting down his cheeks. "Why do you have to go?" he said through whimpers. Squeezing his hand tighter, he lowered his face and kissed Tanyth's cheek.

"I'm sorry for leaving you, for abandoning you when I'd given you so much hope. I was scared and not ready… but I realise now that I was, that I am. Because you make me ready. You give me that feeling of protection and safety." He wiped a tear from his face just as it hit his lip. "I still remember what you said to me in the inn, you know… Love is when you feel safe. Love is when you feel you can tell them everything and not be afraid to leave out any details. Love is when I'm with you, Tanyth."

AIWEN SMILED THROUGH HIS PAIN, MASKING HIS sorrow *for* his last moments. He would've told him to never guard his true emotions, but Aiwen had to do this. Tanyth's last sight couldn't be Aiwen's anguish. So he wiped the last trace of tears from his face and placed his other hand in Tanyth's grip. He relished in his touch, knowing it would be the last time he would feel him. Tanyth's eyes opened and shut over and over, like he was fighting to stay awake.

"Don't fight just for me, Tan," Aiwen mumbled, attempting to mask the falter in his voice. "If it hurts, you can leave. You deserve to be free of your pain, but I won't leave you. I'll stay here until the last moment."

For the first time, something flickered behind Tanyth's dwindling eyes. Behind the myriad of blue, Aiwen felt the happiness ooze from within. He was content, and therefore, so was Aiwen.

Aiwen didn't cry when Tanyth's blinks became further apart. And he didn't scream when his eyes shut and didn't open again. Instead, he squeezed his hand harder in his grasp and forced his own eyes closed. The sight of his dead body shook him too much.

"May the Light protect you and your beautiful soul, Tan. "May I see you again—"

Shuffles behind him startled him, but he soon rested when Alleria resumed her position beside him. Imra and Rosa stood a few lengths behind, respecting their boundaries. Resting her head on Aiwen's shoulders, Alleria cried.

"He's in a better place," Aiwen murmured, draping his arm around her. "He wouldn't want you to cry."

"It's not fair."

"No, it's not."

THEY SAT TOGETHER FOR HOURS, NOT WANTING TO let go of the moment. Sharing stories of Tanyth's life, reminiscing and remembering the man they knew and loved. But eventually, the sun rose, and another day came. The soft light of day showered them all in a warm glow, as if it knew Naesaela was gone. The peace in Malmar was restored, but at what cost.

EPILOGUE

The wind blew harshly upon Alleria Valrona's back as she trudged through the threatening Malmar night. All light gone. Nevertheless, she ventured on through Elorin, Aiwen following close behind her. They had trekked day and night for the past few days after declining the offer to ride the hippogriffs home. They preferred to spend the time together, just how Tanyth would have wanted them to.

Alleria wished to visit her mother's grave in fear of forgetting where it was. She needed to tell her they'd won, even if she couldn't hear. The forest was a maze, but now they felt they had a connection to it. Alleria found she admired the freedom from her power when she entered. She felt free and human. She needed to tell her mother of Tanyth and Alnor's fate. The life after was always a contentious topic for Alleria, but she just hoped her mother would guide Tanyth. He deserved to be happy. He deserved the life he never got. He died in the arms of the ones he loved, but now. He was alone.

Much to her dismay, Aiwen forced her to ask Imra to travel with them, hoping to get to know her further. However, the passing of her uncle had been all too much for her, and she couldn't bear to leave her mother alone. She'd lost her brother and countless friends in Aralva. It was bound to take a toll on even the strongest soul. But it wasn't over for them. Alleria would return to Aralva. She would get her happy ending. Eventually.

AFTER WALKING AIWEN TO HIS DOOR, ALLERIA proceeded straight to the library. The giant oak doors were closed but not locked. She pushed into the enormous frame with her shoulder, wincing at the pressure on the bruises and cuts from the battle. She hadn't realised the wounds were there until after. The adrenaline from the fight must have hidden them.

When she entered, everything was as it was, overturned from the storm, but she expected nothing less. The other citizens of Elorin did not know what happened; they were probably just confused by the library's closing for so long and wondered why the mill wasn't open. Did they have any recollection of what happened to her mother? Living in the dark was hell; she knew the feeling too well. They deserved to know what had transpired. And she would tell them. But not today.

Glass littered the floor, forcing Alleria to skip her way through the halls. She made her way, gradually, to her desk. The feather from her quill still layed on the ground, untouched from weeks ago. She reached for it, careful to avoid any debris, and picked it up, smiling. The feather was the start of it all. Yes, she lost too many people, and her life had been turned upside down, but she'd gained a miraculous ability and met so many she now called friends. That was what her mother would have wanted her to do... look on the bright side of an unpleasant situation; try to find love in the darkest of places. She took her seat and dragged the quill across a fresh sheet of paper. A letter of new beginnings. A letter of truth.

Dear Imra...

AIWEN LAY IN BED, COLD SWEATS HARASSING HIM AS he struggled to drift to sleep. His mind wouldn't stop spiralling with memories of Tanyth and his sudden end. He wasn't to blame, but he felt like he was. Pushing the sheet from his tired frame, he rose to a seated position. He stared at the soft moonlight through the open window. Before, he would have closed the curtains, but now he wanted to see the sky. He wanted to imagine Tanyth looking down at him, making sure he was ok, making fun of everything he did.

He chuckled at the thought and climbed out of bed, knowing he wouldn't sleep anytime soon. The idea of walking to Alleria crossed his mind, but he pushed it away when he remembered the time. She was probably already asleep.

Instead, he strode to the window and perched himself on the sill. His room overlooked the entire square. It was more beautiful than ever, but he was sure his time away was to explain for that. He'd be so homesick.

THE MOONLIGHT CASCADED ITS BRIGHT LIGHT across Elorin, and he tried not to think of his nights staring at the stars with Tanyth. Their time together was short but sweet, a brief memory threatening to be forgotten. But he wouldn't forget their time together, for they were a rose that never blossomed. He promised himself he'd never let the way his curls bounced, and how his icy blue eyes reflected the light as if they were the ocean consign to oblivion. But he knew it was a lie. A lie that would shatter his glass heart all over again once he realised he couldn't quite remember the shade of blonde his hair used to be. Or the depth of his sea blue eyes that he used to get lost in for hours. It was inevitable. And he'd have to deal with that.

Aiwen looked off in the distance, far beyond Elorin, to where the river split and the chasms cried, where the morning light had broken through the horizon and a pinkish glow peeked from behind the trees. His reflection in the window. He ran his hands over his bare chest, carefully avoiding the deep, yet somewhat healed wound from the wolf. He still remembered its harrowing purple eyes and its gnarly jaw that threatened to kill in one bite. Shaking his head free of the thought, he sat and watched the night change into day. However, one thing kept him going, made life worth living. Knowing that another day without his love was another day closer to seeing him again.

PRONUNCIATION GUIDE

CHARACTERS (IN ORDER OF APPEARANCE)

- **Alleria:** A-LEER-EE-a
- **Pyria:** Pi-r-EE-a
- **Tanyth:** Ta-n-IH-th
- **Ayen:** Ai-y-UN
- **Aiwen:** Ai-w-UH-n
- **Naesaela:** N-eye-s-EH-l-a
- **Alnor:** Al-NOR
- **Rosa:** R-OH-sa
- **Imra:** Ih-m-R-a
- **Ruven:** R-OO-v-uu-n
- **Gaelin:** G-AY-l-ih-n

PLACES

- **Malmar:** M-a-l-m-AR
- **Elorin:** Eh-l-OOR-ih-n
- **Aralva:** A-r-a-l-VA
- **Innai:** I-n-EYE
- **River Tarron:** River T-a-r-UH-n
- **Taerel:** T-EYE-r-el

- **Kelgeiros:** K-eh-l-g-EER-o-s

CREATURES

- **Valyuun:** V-al-y-OO-n
- **Nephinae:** N-e-f-i-n-AY

ACKNOWLEDGMENTS

I wrote 98% of this book in my local Starbucks, so first, I thank them for the endless iced caramel macchiatos that definitely **don't** agree with me. However, I still buy them and will continue to.

But for real, as soon as I posted the first video about this book to TikTok, it went wild. The support has been insane. So, this book is for all of you. All of you who interacted with the writing updates, all of you who've pre-ordered my first baby. It's been a joy to write and I can only hope you relate or see yourself somewhere in this crazy ol' story.

I want to thank my editor, Hina, you've been absolutely incredible and so so kind. You understood my story from the get go and transformed it into what it is today.

Jasmine, you were the first ever person I sent a beta copy to and your advice has been so insanely insightful. But above all, you've been a great friend who I can talk to, whether it is author stuff or not.

Char, you have been the MOST supportive person when it comes to writing this book. The constant voice notes, ideas, general encouragement—I wouldn't have finished this without you.

Celine, I still go over my notes from our three hour FaceTime after you finished the book—you went IN. But it made this story so much better than it was and I couldn't be more grateful.

I also want to thank all my other beta readers for your honest, but needed, feedback.

Thank you Melissa for bringing Malmar to life with your beautiful map.

And thank you to Ben. Your cover illustration was more incredible than I could have imagined. You brought one of my favourite scenes in the book to life. I can't wait to work with you again.

Finally, I want to thank my friends and family. My parents, for helping this far-off dream become a reality. My nan, for reading the book, despite it not being written by James Patterson or Danielle Steel. My auntie, even if you never finished the copy I gave you… lol. I know you love me, really.

And to the readers, I can't wait for you to see what's next—I think you're going to really like it.

ABOUT THE AUTHOR

A Tempest of Emerald Dream is William J Wood's debut novel. He describes the book as a classic quest fantasy but twenty twenty two-ified. You can find him primarily on TikTok expressing his love for books and writing at @billreads. If it wasn't obvious, he goes by Billy most of the time <3

instagram.com/billreadslol
goodreads.com/billywood

Printed in Poland
by Amazon Fulfillment
Poland Sp. z o.o., Wrocław

89431959R00214